ENHANCING ORGANIZATIONAL EFFECTIVENESS IN ADULT AND COMMUNITY EDUCATION

The Professional Practices in Adult Education and Human Resource Development Series explores issues and concerns of practitioners who work in the broad range of settings in adult and continuing education and human resource development.

The books are intended to provide information and strategies on how to make practice more effective for professionals and those they serve. They are written from a practical viewpoint and provide a forum for instructors, administrators, policy makers, counselors, trainers, managers, program and organizational developers, instructional designers, and other related professionals.

Editorial correspondence should be sent to

Editor
Professional Practices Series
Krieger Publishing Company
P.O. Box 9542
Melbourne, FL 32902-9542

ENHANCING ORGANIZATIONAL EFFECTIVENESS IN ADULT AND COMMUNITY EDUCATION

Gary J. Dean
Peter J. Murk
Tony Del Prete

KRIEGER PUBLISHING COMPANY
MALABAR, FLORIDA
2000

Original Edition 2000

Printed and Published by
KRIEGER PUBLISHING COMPANY
KRIEGER DRIVE
MALABAR, FLORIDA 32950

Copyright © 2000 by Gary J. Dean, Peter J. Murk and Tony Del Prete

> FROM A DECLARATION OF PRINCIPLES JOINTLY ADOPTED BY A COM-
> MITTEE OF THE AMERICAN BAR ASSOCIATION AND A COMMITTEE OF
> PUBLISHERS:
>
> This publication is designed to provide accurate and authoritative information in
> regard to the subject matter covered. It is sold with the understanding that the
> publisher is not engaged in rendering legal, accounting, or other professional service.
> If legal advice or other expert assistance is required, the services of a competent
> professional person should be sought.

Library of Congress Cataloging-in-Publication Data

Dean, Gary J.
     Enhancing organizational effectiveness in adult and community
education / Gary J. Dean, Peter J. Murk, Tony Del Prete. — Original ed.
     p.   cm. — (Professional practices in adult education and human
resource development series)
     Includes bibliographical references and index.
     ISBN 1-57524-001-7 (alk. paper)
     1. Adult education—United States—Administration. 2. Community
education—United States—Administration. I. Murk, Peter J., 1942–
II. Del Prete, Tony, 1958– III. Title. IV. Series.

LC5225.A34 D43 2000
374'.973—dc21
                                                      99-088738

10   9   8   7   6   5   4   3   2

CONTENTS

Experiential Learning Activities

PREFACE

The challenges facing adult and community education organizations and educators have never been as great as they are now—and will continue to be in the future. A host of issues looms on the horizon including where to find dynamic leaders, funding, and volunteers.

Currently, many books and videotapes are available to help individuals and organizations become more productive. Other resources help us to develop a positive self-image. Still others enable us to explore dreams, ambitions, and career options for living a more satisfying life.

We designed this book to be useful from multiple perspectives. On one level it acts as an improvement handbook for both individuals and organizations. On another level, the book is a handy resource and reference for meeting today's organizational challenges. And on a third level, the book is a guide for leaders and organizations entering the new world of adult and community education in the twenty-first century.

The idea for this book occurred during a discussion about activities used in the classroom to enhance learning. We discovered that we shared a passion for active learning and learner involvement. We decided to combine text and experiential learning activities both to promote individual professional development and to enhance organizational effectiveness in adult and community education.

In essence, we developed this book as a supplement and resource for enhancing existing programs and organizational efforts. Each chapter addresses a different challenge and yet all are linked by a common goal: to make organizations stronger and more effective in their daily operations and their ongoing improvement efforts.

This book acts as a handy reference to proven tools and techniques that make the individual's job more manageable, the work of associates more satisfying, and the organization itself a better place to work. The suggestions and exercises can be adapted to meet an organization's specific needs, and the examples may inspire the creation of other unique simulations for the organization.

Each chapter explores a topic of vital interest to many adult and community education organizations today. The general approach is to present a topic and supplement it with one or more experiential learning activities. The activities at the end of each chapter help readers internalize the information presented in the text and apply the information to their own professional and organizational situations.

The book can be used in several ways. First, it can be read for information. In this sense each chapter acts as a primer on the topic addressed. Second, the activities can be used in classes or workshops for training adult and community educators. The preferred method, however, is that a group of coworkers will use the text and accompanying activities to explore topics of interest as they attempt to grow professionally and enhance their organization's effectiveness. We believe the book will be most effective when employees of an adult or community education organization can also act as a learning group. In small agencies, for example, the entire staff may learn together as they engage in the experiential learning activities. In larger organizations, the groups may be identified by departments, teams, or people with common learning interests and goals.

Two topics are addressed in Chapter 1. The primary topic describes the connection between individual professional development and organizational enhancement. The second presents a model for experiential learning in organizations. The model is used throughout the book to organize the learning activities. Each learning activity has five stages.

1. Planning, in which the goals of the activity and other planning information are presented

2. Involvement, which includes the instructions to be presented to participants and engagement of the participants in the activity

3. Reflection, generalization, and application, in which participants are encouraged to explore and derive their own meanings from the learning experience

4. Follow-up, which encourages participants to make the connection between the learning activity and the workplace

5. Activity

It will be noted that this organization varies slightly from the model presented in Figure 1.1 which identifies seven stages: planning, involvement, internalization, reflection, generalization, application, and follow-up. Describing more stages makes each part of the experiential learning process more explicit. Fewer stages can often be used in practice to organize an experiential activity.

Chapter 2 is an exploration of strategic planning. It presents foundation materials to help adult and community educators understand what makes an organization work. The case studies included with this chapter focus on intra-organizational dynamics.

Chapter 3 covers grant writing, a necessary tool for many agencies in today's ever-increasing competition for resources. The simulation in this chapter is based on the federal model of a Request for Proposals (RFP) and will show participants how to write grant proposals.

Chapter 4 addresses the concept of leadership. The activities associated with this chapter will help to identify leadership styles and the strengths that can be brought to leadership situations in organizations.

Chapter 5 explores the issues of program planning. The activities within are designed to help readers make the connection between program planning as outlined in the text and as applicable in the real communities where the readers live and work.

Chapter 6 addresses the issues of interagency collaboration and encourages readers to think in broader community-based terms, not just in terms of their agencies. The two activities present powerful experiences for participants to help them reassess their preconceived notions about community.

Chapter 7 focuses on the increasingly important issues of recruiting and managing volunteers. The case study and role play activity will help participants better understand their own volunteer issues.

Chapter 8 is an attempt to bring the book full circle as it reviews the issues of professional development in an organizational context. This chapter allows readers to focus attention on their own professional development and how it relates to that of others in their organizations, as well as how it contributes to their organizations' effectiveness.

Clearly, the book cannot be all things to all people and all organizations. However, it is our intent to provide a starting point for individuals, teams, and organizations in adult and community education by allowing them to explore the critical issues with which they are faced. We hope that the book and the readers are successful.

ACKNOWLEDGMENTS

This book has truly been a collaborative effort. Many people have contributed to its completion. Gary Dean wishes to thank his students, who have wittingly and unwittingly contributed with their ideas garnered through thoughtful comments and compelling discussions. He also wishes to thank Pat Dietrich for her literature review which contributed to Chapter 2. And, as always, nothing is possible without Sandy, Jess, Jenn, Penny, and Glennie.

Peter Murk wishes to acknowledge many colleagues and friends who contributed to this effort. Thanks are extended to Ross Van Ness, Jim McElhinney, and Joe Rawlings, who served as special mentors. Peter also wishes to acknowledge Jackie Nickerson, Elaine Weber, Howard Hickey, and Lou Romano from Michigan State University who shared in his experiential learning process and in its creative design. To Drs. Clyde M. Campbell and Don Nickerson from Michigan State University, a special thank you in memoriam. To all his colleagues in the Educational Leadership Department, but especially Bobby Malone, Jean Flemming, Terry Wiedmar, Ted Kowalski, and Joe McKinney, who shouted encouragement and gave support. To the doctoral students, but especially Jeff Walls, who helped develop the Planning Wheel, and to Juan Carlos, Tracy, A. K., Pierre, Matt, Rod, and Cheryl who offered advice. To Michael Galbraith, the editor-in-chief, a special thanks for his encouragement and support, and to Mary Roberts at Krieger Publishing, who made our project even better. And finally, Peter wishes to thank his family, Dotty, Karen, Diane, and Laurie Michelle, for their patience, kindness, and support. Thank you, everyone!

Tony Del Prete thanks his family, friends, and colleagues for their ongoing support of all his writing endeavors. He also recognizes Drs. Dandeneau, Fontaine, Witchel, and Worzbyt for their time, mentoring, and support during his graduate studies at Indiana University of Pennsylvania. Lastly, he is grateful to Drs. Dean and Murk for sharing their wisdom, knowledge, expertise, and most importantly, their friendship while participating in the writing of this book.

In addition to the people listed above, the following individuals have written or helped in the development of the learning activities and provided permission for use of their work in this book.

Taking the Lead: Informal Group Leadership Assessment; Follow the Leader: Rotating Discussion Leaders; and Making Cents: Conflict Resolution were written by Jackie Nickerson who gave her permission for their use in the book.

Help, Inc.: A Case Study of Changing Times and Values; The Perfect Adult and Community Education Organization; EDCILL Grant Writing Simulation; and the Professional Development Plan were developed by Gary Dean. Thanks to Nancy Norberg for her extensive help in developing the EDCILL Grant Writing Simulation. Also, thanks to Archie Tinelli, Georgiana Jones, Joe Norden Jr., and the Fall 1997 Monroeville class of AC 620 for their help in revising and refining Help, Inc.

Sandstone Community Case Study; Easturbia Case Study; and Westville, U.S.A.: A Case Study in Community Education were developed by Peter Murk.

Community Dilemma and A Course of a Different Color: Group Dynamics Role Play were developed by Ross Van Ness who gave his permission for their use in the book.

Volunteer Management Dilemma was written by Joe Levine and Jim Snoddy who gave their permission for its use in this book.

Unfortunately, despite extensive efforts, the author of Join the Club: Community Exercise could not identified. This activity was included because it is stimulating and appropriate for the topic addressed in the chapter.

Ethan Janove gave his permission for the use of Figure 6.1.

THE AUTHORS

Gary J. Dean is Associate Professor of Adult and Community Education at Indiana University of Pennsylvania (IUP). He received his doctorate in adult education from The Ohio State University in 1987. His M.A. was also earned at Ohio State in 1982, and he graduated from Miami University (Ohio) with a B.S. in education in 1972.

Before starting at IUP in 1987 Dean worked as a drug and alcohol rehabilitation counselor and education specialist for the U.S. Army, a career counselor, counselor supervisor, a trainer of career counselors for the Ohio Bureau of Employment Services, and as a graduate assistant developing training programs at the National Center for Research in Vocational Education.

Dean's concentration in experiential learning is based on his experience in developing training materials, including a comprehensive training program for career counselors at the Ohio Bureau of Employment Services and for the U.S. Department of Defense. Further, he has extensive consulting experience with community agencies, hospitals, government, and private industry.

Dean's activities include directing a Student Literacy Corps project, working with displaced workers, authoring *Designing Instruction for Adult Learners* (1994), and serving as coeditor for the *PAACE Journal of Lifelong Learning*, the professional journal of the Pennsylvania Association for Adult Continuing Education.

Peter J. Murk is Professor of Adult and Community Education and Director of the master's degree program in executive development for the public service with the Department of

Educational Studies at Ball State University. He received his Ph.D. degree from Michigan State University in higher education with cognate areas in educational administration and adult and community education and did postdoctoral work in leadership training and financial planning as a Lilly Fellow at Georgetown University in 1976. Prior to that he received his M.A. degree (1971) from Eastern Michigan University in community school administration and his B.A. degree (1965, with honors) from Northern Michigan University in sociology and social science teaching.

Murk has spent more than 30 years in education as a high school teacher of social studies and Latin; elementary school administrator (community school director) in Flint, Michigan; instructor and community development trainer with the Mott Institute for Community Improvement at Michigan State University; consultant for The Institute for Community Education Development; administrator with The School of Continuing Education; coordinator for the Ball State University summer Elderhostel Programs; and executive secretary for the Indiana Association for Adult and Continuing Education. Murk was honored by former Governor Orr as a "Sagamore of the Wabash," and is listed in *Who's Who in the Midwest*. He served as a visiting senior lecturer with Westminster College, Oxford, England, and as a visiting professor with the University of Georgia and Indiana University of Pennsylvania. He was recently the Ball State Delegate Leader to China and the Far East, and most recently a traveler to the Middle East.

He has written more than 30 articles on topics such as community leadership and visioning, in-service training, program planning, interagency cooperation, volunteers, and assessment techniques for *Adult Learning, The Community Education Journal, Economic Development Review*, and *Training and Development Journal*. He has presented research papers on adult and community education topics at regional, national, and international conferences. He has designed training programs and conducted over 70 training seminars on such topics as management skills improvement and staff development, community leadership training, and grant writing skills for professional and community groups. He serves on the Board of Directors and reviewer for the Midwest Research-to-Practice Conference, and he has been a member of the Commission of Professors of Adult Education and AAACE since 1984.

Tony Del Prete is a guidance counselor in the Greater Latrobe School District and owner of a writing, marketing, and consulting company in Pittsburgh, Pennsylvania. He received an M.Ed. in counseling education from Indiana University of Pennsylvania in 1997 and was the recipient of the Outstanding Student Award. Prior to that he graduated from the University of Pittsburgh in 1982 with a B.A. in English literature.

Del Prete has worked in the field of human resources for more than 15 years, specializing in training and development that encompasses interviewing and hiring skills training, drug and alcohol awareness-building, assessment center simulations, and customer service programs. In the positions of technical writer, editor, and marketing manager, he has developed a range of training materials and peripherals for companies including Citibank, Los Angeles Unified School District, Edy's Grand Ice Cream, and Florida Schools.

He has edited and promoted several business and self-help books, including *Zapp! The Lightning of Empowerment*, *Lincoln on Leadership*, and *Controlling Stress in the Workplace*. He is currently an at-large editor for Lee Shore Literary Agency in Pittsburgh, Pennsylvania, editing a variety of fiction and non-fiction manuscripts. His first book, *Where in the World? Travels and Travails in Search of the Good Life*, was published in 1996.

Del Prete has written articles for a variety of magazines, journals, and newspapers, including *Training & Development Journal*, *Our Children*, *Gifted Child Today*, and *The School Counselor*. He was also writer/editor for the Pennsylvania School Counselor Association's 1997 conference program and assistant editor for the 1996 *PAACE Journal of Lifelong Learning*, the professional journal of the Pennsylvania Association for Adult Continuing Education. He is in *Who's Who Among America's Educators 2000*.

CHAPTER 1

Experiencing Professional and Organizational Development

In no country in the world have the principles of association been more successfully used or applied to a greater multitude of objects than in America. Besides the permanent associations which are established by law . . . a vast number of others are formed and maintained by the agency of primary individuals. . . . In the United States, associations are established to promote the public safety, commerce, industry, morality and religion. There is no end which the human will despairs of attaining through the combined power of individuals united in a society.

Alexis de Tocqueville, *Democracy in America*

This book is based on several assumptions about individual and organizational development. First, professionals in adult and community education can and want to develop as professionals. In addition, individual professional development can contribute to organizational effectiveness. That is, if the people who work in an organization are better trained and prepared to do their jobs, then the organization will be more efficient and effective in delivering its services.

Professional development can be accomplished by both individual and group means, but is most effective for organizational effectiveness when group learning is involved. Learning in groups has the added benefit of helping to create positive group cohesiveness and a dynamic which can carry over onto the job after training. The participants gain not only knowledge and skills, but also important insights on how to function as a team.

The final assumption about individual development is a

well-tested axiom in adult education: learning is most effective when it is active and participatory. When learners are actively involved in the process, then they can integrate new learning into their understanding of the world and have greater opportunities for changes in outlooks, perspectives, and behavior on the job.

To that end, the message of this book is simple and clear: implement active group learning centered around issues that deal directly with organizational enhancement. The purpose of this book is to engage coworkers as learners so that they can examine their own place in the organization, better understand the nature and dynamics of their organization, develop their talents and skills as educators and leaders, and develop a better ability to work with others in their organization to accomplish its mission.

The chapters in this book follow a logical progression. In Chapter 2 the readers are engaged in strategic planning. The first part of this process is understanding how the organization is "organized." In effect, this "taking stock" will help readers identify and understand salient points regarding how and why the organization in which they work functions. Building upon this assessment, readers are walked through the strategic planning steps. The next logical activity for most organizations to consider is acquiring resources. In Chapter 3, the specific resource acquisition strategy emphasized is grant writing. Developing leadership skills follows as a necessary part of enhancing organizational effectiveness and is addressed in Chapter 4. Since many if not most adult and community education organizations deliver their services through "programs" that they offer, Chapter 5 addresses this function. Reaching out into the community is an important and necessary step for most organizations. Here this is accomplished through developing interagency cooperation (Chapter 6) and recruiting and managing volunteers (Chapter 7). Finally, the process of professional and organizational development is brought full circle in Chapter 8 where some ideas for continuing professional and organizational development are broached. In reality these activities would not usually be sequential. This approach to the content and organization of this book, however, flows logically from first examining the organization to planning to resource acquisition to leading to developing community outreach. The process is ever evolving and widening and the impact is ever expanding.

In this chapter, a broader picture of professional development is discussed to lay a foundation for the book. The link between professional and organizational development is addressed, as is the nature of experiential learning in developing activities for the book. A model of experiential learning, which is used for the organization of learning activities, is also presented.

PROFESSIONAL DEVELOPMENT

Galbraith and Zelenak (1989) outline the major approaches to professional development in adult education. They focus on professional development of practitioners in adult education and identify several forms it can take: on-the-job training, in-service training, and formal graduate degree programs in adult education. They state that the purpose of such training is for practitioners in adult education to "acquire the knowledge, skills, attitudes, and behaviors needed to achieve the purposes of their jobs and to improve their performance" (p. 126). Implied in this definition, although not stated directly, is that the organization in which the practitioners work will also be improved through such professional development activities.

Brockett (1989) adds another dimension to professional development in his discussion of professional associations in which adult educators can participate. He points out that professional associations contribute to individuals, to the field, and to society. Collins (1991) takes the idea of professional development one step further. He states that training in technical competence in job skills is important but by itself insufficient. He adds two additional functions. First, training in technical competence is more effective when it is situation specific and not presented in "pre-packaged curriculum formats" (p. 90). Second, adult educators must develop a sense of "communicative competence as an integral dimension of training [which] calls for the provision of opportunities for trainees to [discuss] their work and the work context, situating it within the larger society" (p. 88). This dialogue among coworkers will lead to what Collins refers to as "questioning what's taken for granted," incorporating critical reflection into the everyday activities of adult and community educators.

LINKING PROFESSIONAL DEVELOPMENT TO ORGANIZATIONAL DEVELOPMENT

The link between professional development and organizational effectiveness is at the same time both obvious and obscure. The obvious connection is that practitioners who are more knowledgeable and skilled can perform their jobs better and, thus, the organizations in which they work will better be able to carry out their goals and functions. The obscure part of the connection between professional development and organizational effectiveness is how the improvement of individual employees actually contributes to organizational efficacy. The assumption often made is analogous to Bergevin's (1967) portrayal of progressive thought regarding the value of adult education in society. He claimed better education produces better citizens, which results in a better society. The problem with this assumption is that the effect of individual improvement on the organization is often long term and can be diminished by the organizational structure, membership, and culture.

Many organizations in adult and community education are dependent upon immediate improvements in effectiveness if they are to thrive, or in some cases survive. Continued funding, often on a year-to-year basis, is often contingent upon outcome criteria such as improvements in learning levels of participants, number of learners who take and/or pass the GED, numbers participating in programs, or job placement and retention rates. These kinds of goals demand an approach to organizational effectiveness that is focused on the immediate operations of the organization. The link between professional development and organizational effectiveness must be made more explicit if it is to serve these immediate organizational needs. This is accomplished through three basic approaches used in this book:

1. Initiate professional development in the workplace instead of taking individuals off site for training.

2. Center the learning around organizational enhancement issues.

3. Create a framework that encourages coworkers to critically examine themselves as professionals as well as their interactions and effectiveness as part of the larger organization.

EXPERIENTIAL LEARNING

Experiential learning is a term used to indicate learning through doing. Its common use in adult education has been to describe internships and long-term experiential projects in which students engage as part of a larger, formal learning program. The term is used here in a broader sense to describe all learning that is derived from active engagement of the learner. In this sense, we are using experiential learning in the same way as Dewey (1938) who describes the dual nature of experiences in learning. He emphasizes both the environmental aspects of experience and the personal or internal aspects of experience, and emphasizes the need to bridge these two components. This dual nature of experience is what gives experiential learning its power. Experiential learning is most effective when previous knowledge can be linked with current learning and future applications of that learning in a way that allows the person to fully integrate the past, present, and future.

Kolb (1984) expands on Dewey's ideas of experience and education by offering the following definition of learning: "Learning is the process whereby knowledge is created through the transformation of experience" (p. 38). This definition emphasizes the role of experience in learning. Kolb explains his definition further by stating: (1) the definition emphasizes the process of adaptation and learning as opposed to outcomes, (2) knowledge is a transformation process, being continually created and recreated, (3) learning transforms experience in both its objective and subjective forms, and (4) understanding the nature of knowledge is critical to understanding the nature of learning. This definition, while it goes beyond what is intended in this book, lays the foundation for the approach to learning emphasized here.

The dual nature of experience is at the heart of experiential learning as it is used in the exercises contained in this book. Learning occurs as an objective experience, that is, it incorporates the prior experience of the learners and the organizational structure and context in which the learning occurs. Learning is also subjective, however, in that each learner experiences activities differently and arrives at independent conclusions about the topic being learned. It is the process of making these differences explicit in shared communication among the learners that offers the greatest chance of not only learning from one's own experience, but from that of others as well.

A PROCESS MODEL OF EXPERIENTIAL LEARNING

The model used to develop the learning activities in this book is displayed in Figure 1.1. A process model of experiential learning, expanded from Dean (1993a), is based on stages adapted from Pfeiffer and Jones (1983). The model assumes a group of learners working together under the guidance of a group leader or facilitator who assumes a leadership role in helping the group get involved in the learning activity, process the learning, and apply the learning to activities on the job. The model consists of seven stages, each explained with three different functions: the leader's role regarding the content and process of the learning activity; the leader's role regarding the process of conducting the activity; and the learners' role and level of involvement in the activity.

The seven stages of experiential learning in the model are

not static or linear and may be revisited throughout the learning process. In the **planning** stage, the leader assesses the learners' readiness to participate in the activity (either formally or informally), and develops and prepares the learning activity. In the following chapters, activities and materials are fully developed and presented to help plan for common workplace issues, but may need to be modified for different organizational contexts.

The second stage, **involvement,** is an important time for the group leader or facilitator. Getting the learners involved by creating a climate for learning has been discussed by a number of authors including Draves (1984), Gagne, Briggs, and Wager (1988), Knox (1986), and Margolis and Bell (1986), each of whom provides insights into how to engage learners in the learning activity. Three central themes can be derived from most of the work on this topic: (1) help the learners to see the relevance of the activity to themselves and their job, (2) be clear about what is to be done, how it is to be done, and who is to do what, and (3) model behavior that contributes to a climate of openness and trust. The last point is critical. If learners do not feel they can participate in the learning activity free of censure, then they are not likely to want to participate at all. If they are forced to participate, then they will play a role to meet the expectations of others instead of openly attempting to learn and grow from the experiences.

The third stage, **internalization,** is when participants are actively engaged in the learning process and doing the learning activity. The role of the leader shifts from one of director during the involvement stage to facilitator for the activity. In this role, the leader encourages participation, clarifies directions, and helps learners maintain motivation to keep on task. This stage is not presented separately in the introduction to the experiential learning activities in this book. It occurs as the participants are engaged in the activity.

The next two stages, **reflection** and **generalization,** are often combined. In these stages, sometimes referred to as debriefing, participants are encouraged to reflect on the learning activity, develop a sense of what it means to them, and make connections between the learning activity and other activities

A Process Model for Experiential Learning in Adult Education

| Stage | Leader/Facilitator | | Learners' Roles |
	Content and Process	Role	
1 **Planning** (Getting Ready)	Assess learners' readiness to participate in experiential learning. Identify desired outcomes and experiential learning methods most appropriate for learners.	Leader prepares the materials and facilities needed for the learning activity.	Not involved at this stage.
2 **Involvement** (Getting Started)	Create a climate for involvement by identifying the relevance of the content, process, and anticipated outcomes of the learning activity for the learners. Create a climate of trust and openness by demonstrating those qualities. Introduce the learning activity and provide clear directions for the learners.	Leader is highly directive at this point, but must be attuned to the reactions and needs of the learners.	Learners should become engaged in the activity at this point; the desired state is one of active interest and involvement.

Stage		Leader	Learners
3 **Internalization** (Learning by Doing)	Help the learners understand the activity by clarifying directions as necessary. Encourage participation when appropriate.	Leader is primarily facilitative at this time, focusing on managing the learning processes. May be directive to help learners keep on task.	Learners are actively engaged in the learning experience at this stage. They are internalizing the messages of the activity by processing the content while they are doing the activity.
4 **Reflection** (Making Meaning)	Clarify concepts learned during the learning activity. Help the learners reflect on the learning activity. Provide encouragement and support for individual learners.	Leader is primarily facilitative, focusing on helping learners process by encouraging discussion. May be directive by providing examples.	Learners strive to derive meaning from the experience. The focus may be on group consensus or individual meaning, or both, depending on the purpose of the activity.
5 **Generalization** (Making Connections)	Help the learners make connections between the learning experience and the rest of the world. For example, provide examples of connections, analogies, or new ways of thinking about making connections.	Leader is primarily facilitative at this stage, focusing on helping learners develop (possibly through brainstorming) connections between the learning activity and their jobs, communities, etc.	Learners may work independently or in small groups to make connections.

Figure 1.1 A Process Model for Experiential Learning in Adult Education

| Stage | Leader/Facilitator | | Learners' Roles |
	Content and Process	Role	
6 **Application** (Transfer of Learning)	Provide structure/guidance for learners to transfer learning to real world situations. For example, have learners keep a journal of how they have used what they learned on the job.	Leader's role is primarily supportive at this time, helping the learners to make a successful transfer of learning. Leader must also ensure that learners will be recognized for successes and not be penalized for mistakes made when applying new learning.	Learners must be able to use the connections they made in the previous stage and apply their new learning on the job or in their communities, etc.
7 **Follow-up** (Assessment and Planning)	Assess the learners' abilities to apply their new learning. Use the information gained from assessment to guide individual learners and plan for future learning activities.	Leader's role is primarily directive at this time and may involve the use of formal assessment tools (tests, performance evaluations, etc.) or informal evaluation procedures (such as observation and discussion with the learners).	Not involved at this stage.

Figure 1.1 A Process Model for Experiential Learning in Adult Education (Continued)

such as job functions. The important aspect of these stages is that learners must make their own meaning and connections; they must not be told what the meanings and connections are. Again, the leader is primarily a facilitator in these stages, allowing the learners to develop their own sense of what can be learned from the activity as well as how it applies to their jobs.

In the sixth stage, **application**, participants are encouraged to apply what they have learned to their jobs in a concrete and realistic way. This stage may be accomplished in many different ways. For example, learners may brainstorm ways their jobs or the organization can be improved based on what they have learned. They may decide to develop a long-term approach to developing new methods or procedures for the organization. Even restructuring the organization may be seen as a desirable outcome if the learners believe that is appropriate. The application stage is combined with the reflection and generalization stages in the presentation of the experiential learning activities in this book. In practice, the discussion following a learning activity will often yield all three of these learning outcomes simultaneously.

Follow-up is the last stage of the learning activity and is inherent in any good learning situation. The leader assesses the impact of changed behavior and/or activities on the job while learners provide feedback regarding the success of implementing new ideas adopted as a result of the learning activity. This stage lays the groundwork for future learning activities and subsequent changes in the organization.

SUMMARY

Alone, each of these stages can influence an individual's development; together, they can have a multiplying effect that reaches throughout the organization. Yet, as noted from the description of the stages in the experiential model, there must be a basic assumption of openness and trust between leadership and professionals and among the professionals themselves within the organization. This assumption is imperative for this approach to enhancing professional development and organizational effectiveness to work. A climate of distrust or despair will render this or any other approach ineffective.

Preliminary to any learning activities, members of an organization may want to engage in team-building strategies to create an environment of teamwork, cooperation, group cohesiveness, and trust. The following books contain group activities and processes that can contribute to the development of group openness and trust. Of particular note is *CReST* by Francesco Sofo (1995) for developing group reflectivity and critical thinking skills. The group processes and learning activities in these references may be useful: *Team Games for Trainers* (Nilson, 1993), *Games We Should Play in School* (Aycox, 1985), *Games Trainers Play* (Scannell & Newstrom, 1980), and *More Games Trainers Play* (Scannell & Newstrom, 1983).

CHAPTER 2

Implementing Strategic Planning

Organizations in adult and community education are faced with many decisions. Two vital questions are, What programs shall we run? How can we improve relationships with other organizations and the community at large? The answers to these questions are critical for growth. This chapter focuses on strategic planning, a framework for understanding and managing the dynamics of organizational growth. First, strategic planning is defined and the process outlined, followed by a discussion on how to get organized and gain commitment for strategic planning. Assessing internal and external environmental factors is then described. Next, the special considerations of community education organizations are discussed. The final sections deal with making decisions and implementing the plan.

THE STRATEGIC PLANNING PROCESS

Simerly (1987a) defines strategic planning as "a process that gives attention to (1) designing, (2) implementing, and (3) monitoring plans for improving the organization decision-making process" (p. 1). Another way to look at it is that strategic planning involves assessing the organization, making decisions regarding desired directions of the organization for the future, and implementing and monitoring those decisions.

Indeed, strategic planning is a systematic process that can be contrasted to an intuitive process of decision making and planning that relies on the leader's knowledge and skill in assessing and thinking ahead. It is not that an intuitive approach to planning is necessarily ineffective, but more that a systematic approach offers certain benefits. At its best, strategic planning becomes embedded in the daily routine of the organization; it becomes part of the organizational culture. All members of the organization commit to the process which leads to a sense of ownership in the organization and a feeling of control over the future of the organization.

Based on the review of the literature, Simerly (1987b) identified seven steps in strategic planning:

1. Conduct a management audit. This "serves to analyze the present situation of the organization" (p. 14). The management audit should identify the organization's strengths and weaknesses, windows of opportunity, what should be changed and why, and how difficult it will be to implement the desired changes.

2. Clarify values, which consists of identifying the culture of the organization.

3. Develop a mission statement for the organization.

4. Establish goals and objectives for the organization. Goals are general statements of desired outcomes, whereas objectives are measurable statements that give specificity to the goals.

5. Develop an action plan. The plan should identify how and when the goals and objectives will be realized and who is responsible.

6. Conduct a reality test of the goals and objectives. In this step, members of the organization reflect on their plan to determine whether it is feasible given resource constraints and other limitations the organization faces.

7. Develop feedback systems. In the final step processes are put in place that allow monitoring of progress and corrections if needed during implementation of the plan.

For the purposes of many smaller, more informal organizations Simerly's seven steps can be condensed into a more manageable five steps. The steps are outlined here and described in further detail.

1. Getting organized and gaining commitment

2. Assessing internal assets and liabilities

3. Assessing the external environment

4. Making decisions to identify future directions

5. Implementing and assessing the plan

Activity 2.3, Westville, U.S.A.: A Case Study in Community Education, provides an opportunity to apply strategic planning on a community-wide basis including all of the steps outlined above.

GETTING ORGANIZED AND GAINING COMMITMENT

The first step in strategic planning is getting organized and gaining commitment. It requires doing research and selling the idea to the administrators and staff of the organization. The project manager needs to get buy-in from management because if they're not willing and/or able to follow through with implementing decisions, reduced morale and negative backlash may result among employees.

Another aspect of gaining commitment is to determine which members of the organization will be involved in the planning. A larger organization may need to work through committees that use representatives of the various departments and constituencies in the organization. Employing a committee of the whole may work better in a smaller organization. In either case, the decisions about who will participate are critical. Department representatives must be capable of handling issues at hand and be respected by employees and management alike. Lack of credibility will have a negative impact on overall success.

Typically, several committees are convened to focus on the

different aspects of strategic planning. Some concerns often addressed in nonprofit organizations include organizational structure, organizational culture and climate, fund-raising and resource acquisition, mission and philosophy, public relations and marketing, and collaboration and competition with other organizations. These issues are not always addressed in the same way; many organizations prefer to divide the topic areas differently. However the committees are defined, there are usually two broad areas of assessment that provide information for decision making on a range of activities: internal (which includes organizational structure, culture, and climate) and external (which comprises fund-raising and resource acquisition, public relations and marketing, collaboration and competition with other organizations, and environmental scanning).

Acquiring information about these two areas is fundamental to any strategic planning. One model for strategic planning is SWOT, which stands for Strengths, Weaknesses, Opportunities, and Threats (Schmidt, 1987). The first two areas are assessments of internal functions, while the second two assess the environment outside the organization.

ASSESSING INTERNAL ASSETS AND LIABILITIES

Three general areas in an organization can be assessed: the purpose of the organization, the organizational structure, and organizational climate and culture. Each of these areas presents different challenges for trying to understand the dynamics that underlie how and why an organization exists.

Assessing the Purpose of the Organization

A basic question to ask is, Why does your organization exist (other than to provide you with employment!)? This question can be rephrased as, What is your organization's basic purpose? and Who benefits from the existence of your organization? Blau and Scott (1962) conducted a review of the literature to arrive at a classification system for organizations that addresses the central issue of why an organization exists. They asked the simple question, Who is the primary beneficiary from the existence of the organization? Having asked the question, Blau and Scott arrived at four types of organizations.

1. Business concerns, whose primary beneficiary are the owners. Examples of this type of organization in adult education are proprietary schools that cater to an adult population such as some business schools, technical schools, or high school degree completion programs.

2. Mutual benefit associations. Here the primary beneficiaries are the members of the organization itself. Examples include professional associations and cooperatives.

3. Service organizations where external clients are served by the organization. This is the category to which many adult and community educators can relate, often perceiving themselves as service providers. For example, running an adult basic education program or offering continuing professional education can be viewed as providing services to specific groups of adult learners.

4. Commonwealth organizations, which service all of society. Examples of commonwealth organizations are the military services and police departments. These types of organizations do not necessarily serve any particular client group, but their general services are beneficial to all members of society.

The usefulness of Blau and Scott's organization classification scheme is twofold. First, asking the question "Who benefits?" will help identify primary beneficiaries of the organization, giving clarity and focus to the primary mission of the organization. Second, a discussion among the members of the organization can reveal differences of opinion regarding who the primary beneficiaries of the organization are.

One area of contention among adult and community educators is whether they provide a service or work for commonwealth organizations. Although service organizations have a narrower purpose than commonwealth organizations, some organizations may see themselves serving both purposes. For example, some adult basic education organizations help adults become better readers, which, in turn, helps them to become more productive members of society, which is seen as benefiting society at large. When this is the case, it is helpful to make both purposes explicit in the organization's mission statement. It is equally important, however, to distinguish between primary and secondary beneficiaries. It is difficult to maintain the energy and acquire the resources to serve two primary beneficiaries and attempting to do so will often result in a loss of focus in the organization.

Coming to an understanding of the basic purpose of an organization is just the beginning. This information can be put to useful purpose in the construction of a mission statement. One of the common outcomes of strategic planning is developing or rewriting the mission statement for the organization. This statement is designed to accomplish several things:

- It is a public statement of what the organization is about.
- It reminds members of the organization of the overall purpose of the organization as they go about their daily activities
- It serves as a point of departure for future modifications of the mission statement.

Some organizations develop both a mission and a vision statement. The vision statement is generally shorter than the mission statement and serves to identify the key attributes of an organization, its primary clientele, and what the organization does. In contrast, the mission statement can be longer (although brevity is a plus) and serves to identify in more detail the primary goals of the organization and what the organization will do to meet them. Usually mission statements (1) address the purpose or major goals of the organization, (2) indicate what is unique about the organization in contrast to others providing similar services, and (3) present a statement of commitment or promise that reflects the core values of the organization. Activity 2.1, The Perfect Adult and Community Education Organization, further explores the importance of mission statements. In the activity, readers will learn that there is more than one way to achieve the goals identified in a mission statement, and that none of them are perfect.

Assessing Organizational Structure

As organizations have evolved and developed over the decades, so too have theories and philosophies about how they should be structured, organized, and managed. Scott (1981) identified three perspectives for viewing organizations: rational systems, natural systems, and open systems. The first is the **rational systems perspective**. Scott defines *rational* in a narrow or technical sense as "a series of actions organized in such a way as to lead to predetermined goals with maximum efficiency. Thus, rationality refers not to the selection of goals but to their implementation" (pp. 57–58).

One hallmark of a rational systems perspective is formalization in organizations. Scott states that "a structure is formalized to the extent that the rules governing behavior [on the job] are precisely and explicitly formulated and to the extent that roles and role relations are prescribed independently of the personal attributes of individuals occupying positions in the structure" (pp. 59–60).

Two elements of formalized organizations are job descriptions and organization charts. All organizations can be viewed through a rational systems perspective. Many adult and community educators may take umbrage at this description of rationality in their organizations, claiming that their organizations are humane and that people drive the organization, not charts or job descriptions. This view may be especially true in smaller organizations where personalities and interpersonal relationships are often the dominating factor governing how the organization's mission is accomplished. Even in the case of small, less formal organizations, however, it is important to note that there is a process for making decisions; that is, there is a structure in which some person by virtue of his or her position in the organization is responsible. Also, it is important to note that while people bring a position to life and give it meaning, there is usually a position description which is the basis for their actions. Much the way an actor follows a script, bringing the role to life, so too must workers use job descriptions as their scripts to bring jobs to life.

Organization charts serve the purpose of providing a picture of how the organization is supposed to function, at least on paper. As depicted in Figure 2.1, there are usually four kinds of relationships which can be identified through an organizational chart: staff, line, functional, and affiliative. Line relationships are characterized by the solid lines. They indicate relationships of authority: who reports to whom and who makes decisions for different areas in the organization. Staff relationships are characterized by double horizontal lines in the figure and represent the people who work together to accomplish the various tasks in the organization. Typically, people on the same level in the chart have a similar amount of status, position power, and authority to make decisions. Functional relationships are those identified by the heavy solid lines and represent special relations necessary to accomplish specific functions or short-term projects. Affiliative relationships are designated by the broken line and connote an informal or advisory association where one position, such as an advisory board or review panel, provides input but does not have authority to enforce its decisions or recommendations.

Organizational structure may be assessed by reviewing the formal structure of the organization and asking, How well is the current structure helping the organization accomplish its mission? Structure is usually viewed through organization charts and position descriptions. Assessing the organizational structure involves reviewing the original and current purpose and functions of each division in the organization. The questions frequently asked include: How much and in what ways has the current purpose of each department shifted from its original purpose? Do the structure and resources of the department allow it to adequately address its current purpose? How well does the current purpose of the department mesh with the purposes of other departments within the organization? How well does

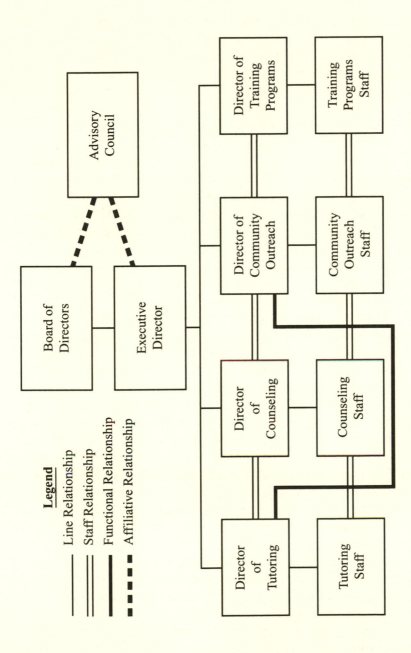

Figure 2.1 Line, staff, functional, and affiliative relationships in an organization

Legend
Line Relationship
Staff Relationship
Functional Relationship
Affiliative Relationship

Board of Directors

Advisory Council

Executive Director

Director of Tutoring

Director of Counseling

Director of Community Outreach

Director of Training Programs

Tutoring Staff

Counseling Staff

Community Outreach Staff

Training Programs Staff

the current purpose of the organization fit in with the overall mission and purpose of the organization? Ultimately, the issue to be addressed through a structural analysis is how the organization can best deliver its services and programs.

Assessing Organizational Climate and Culture

The second perspective identified by Scott (1981) is the **natural systems perspective.** Here, organizations are viewed as collectives or social systems. That is, they are viewed from the behavior of the members of the organization: What do the members believe, feel, and do? In terms of goals, the natural systems perspective identifies the disparity between the stated or intended goals of an organization (rational systems perspective) and the actual or real goals to which people in the organization subscribe (natural systems perspective).

According to the natural systems perspective, the goals of any organization, then, are more complex than the stated goals of the organization in the chart or mission statement. The goals are also reflective of the needs of the people in the organization. For example, interpreting a person's behavior from the perspective of Maslow's (1970) hierarchy of needs leads to an entirely different understanding than simply viewing behavior based on the person's position in an organizational chart. Scott differentiates the rational and natural systems perspectives by stating, "we find it useful to equate formal structures with those norms and behavior patterns that exist regardless of the characteristics of the individual actors. Informal structures are those based on the personal characteristics or resources of the specific participants in the situation" (p. 83).

One of the key ways to understand the natural systems perspective is to look at organizational climate and culture. Assessing the organizational culture and climate is usually much more difficult than assessing organizational structure. Simerly (1991) defined culture as "the underlying fabric in the daily life of the organization. It influences all our actions, determines what risks we will take, what projects we will be willing to initiate, and how we view colleagues" (p. 9). Schein (1985) defined organizational culture as:

> a pattern of basic assumptions—invented, discovered, or developed by a given group as it learns to cope with its problems of external adaptation and internal integration—that has worked well enough to be considered valid and, therefore, to be taught to new members as the correct way to perceive, think, and feel in relation to those problems. (p. 9)

Schein (1985, 1992) also notes that culture consists of three levels: artifacts, espoused values, and basic underlying assumptions. Artifacts are symbols that reflect both the espoused values and underlying assumptions; they include things such as dress, interpersonal behavior, status symbols in the organization, and the physical layout. Espoused values also include what people say, the language they use, and the types of ideals or concepts that members of the organization use to explain or justify their actions. These artifacts illustrate the values and assumptions by displaying what members of the organization think and feel is important. The espoused values of an organization can be understood by listening to the rhetoric used by employees, whereas underlying assumptions are unspoken and often so imbedded in the way of thinking that they go unperceived and unquestioned by employees.

An example of culture in a small, state-funded adult basic education agency may be helpful. Some of the artifacts of the culture are the informal dress, casual and friendly interpersonal behavior, lack of formal indications of status such as titles and deference to superiors, and an atmosphere of camaraderie and mutual support and concern for others. An understanding of the artifacts will quickly give meaning to the espoused values—concern for others, a desire to help, and a sense of "we're all in this together, so we have to work together." Seldom identified and never questioned, the underlying assumptions are (1) the work is far too important to allow the agency to fail, (2) we are a small agency and can only survive if we all work together, and (3) we must be supportive of each other in order to continue. This example illustrates how artifacts, espoused values, and underlying assumptions are all interconnected.

As can easily be seen from the example, assessing organizational culture can be difficult. It often takes outside observers a lengthy period of extensive study to piece together the various aspects of an organization's culture. On the other hand, members of the organization itself are often too close to readily identify aspects of their culture and how it affects the ways in which the organization attempts to accomplish its mission. For these reasons, the assessment of culture in an organization often resides at a superficial level. Organizational culture is further explored in the case study presented in Activity 2.2, Help, Inc., where changes over time and in personnel have caused two distinct cultures to develop in the organization.

ASSESSING THE EXTERNAL ENVIRONMENT

Scott's (1981) third perspective on organizations is the **open systems perspective** in which the organization's environment and the interdependence of organizations within that environment are assessed. All organizations exist in an environment; therefore, understanding that environment and the relationships that exist among organizations in it is crucial to determining how an organization functions. A broad range of factors can be addressed including economic and demographic trends; social shifts; political, legislative, and regulatory changes; and technological advances, as well as the activities of competitors and collaborators (Groff, 1980; Ryan & Townsend, 1992; and Schmidt, 1987).

Environmental scanning is the process of searching for information or trends in the environment that may affect the organization. It has been defined as the "deliberate and systematic identification of emerging or potential trends or forces which may have a substantial impact on the efficiency or effectiveness of an institution in the years to come" (Handy, 1990, p. 7). This would suggest that scanning consists of several processes: identifying key elements in the organization's environment, monitoring them to determine changes and trends, feeding the information gained back into the organization, and using the information for strategic planning (Groff, 1980; Hearn &

Heydinger, 1985). Several environmental scanning models have been developed including PEST—scanning political, economic, social, and technological changes (Esterby-Smith, 1987) and STEEP—scanning social, technological, economical, environmental, and political aspects (Morrison, 1993).

In our assessment here we will focus on several of the external influences on environment. These include the acceptance and task environments, relationships to parent organizations, and funding patterns.

Acceptance and Task Environments

Lauffer (1978) identifies two ways of looking at an organization's environment: the acceptance environment and the task environment. The **acceptance environment** is simply the degree of acceptance or opposition to the adult and community education organization and its function. Lauffer states that there may be acceptance, opposition, or apathy to the organization in three areas: the issues or problems addressed by the organization (such as literacy, vocational training, or professional development), the populations served by the organization, and the services rendered by the organization.

The second environmental analysis recommended by Lauffer is assessing the **task environment**. In this area he recommends that the organizations, agencies, and other entities in the environment of an organization be identified and grouped into four types, or publics: regulators, resource providers, collaborators and competitors, and actual and potential consumers of an organization's programs and services. The nature of the relationship between the organization and each of these publics can be identified and analyzed by asking: Does the relationship need to be changed, strengthened, diminished, or improved? The answers can lead to an enhanced understanding of how an organization is currently functioning in its environment and how the relationships can be maximized to enhance the organization.

Regulators are groups to which an organization is accountable. Government agencies monitoring programs, professional organizations issuing certifications, and local governing boards are all examples of regulators. Resource providers, which may offer tangible or intangible assistance, are the second type of public. Tangible resources include books and materials, money, supplies, facilities, and equipment, which may be donated or supplied at a discount. An example of an intangible resource is association with the "name" of a well-established agency in the community, which lends prestige and credibility to the programs offered by the organization. For example, a community college may team up with a hospital to offer noncredit courses in CPR, first aid, or other health issues, giving programs the increased credibility of two sponsors. Collaborators and competitors are other organizations offering activities similar to the provider organization. In most cases the question is, How can competitors be turned into collaborators? It is much less costly to work with another organization than it is to compete with it for the same turf or learners. The actual and potential consumers of the organization's programs and services are the fourth type of public identified by Lauffer. This category includes the people already participating in the programs, and those the organization would like to attract.

Relationships to Parent Organizations

One of the more enduring classification systems in adult education was developed by Schroeder (1970). In his system, Schroeder asked the question, What is the relationship between the adult education function and the purpose of the parent organization? This system is predicated on the notion that many types of adult education occur in organizations which serve purposes other than adult education. He identified four types of adult education organizations.

In Schroeder's system, Type I agencies are where adult education is the central function of the organization. There often is no parent organization; the adult education function is the whole organization. Examples of organizations in this category include business schools, correspondence schools, and some independent adult basic education agencies.

Type II agencies are those where adult education is a secondary function of an educational institution in which the primary purpose is youth education. Examples include public schools that offer evening adult or community education programs, and many continuing education programs in colleges and universities. The implications of this situation are that in times of scarce resources, the adult education function may be sacrificed by the parent organization. This is often referred to as the theory of marginality.

Type III describes agencies in adult education that are seen as a complementary function of a quasi-educational organization. Examples include libraries, museums, and health and welfare organizations. In Type III agencies, there is usually more than one mission, with adult education identified as one of the primary functions of the organization. For example, a museum may have three primary purposes: conducting research, preservation of artifacts, and providing educational programs.

In Type IV agencies, adult education is a subordinate function in a noneducational organization. Human resources programs in business and industry are a good example of this type of adult education. The parent organization is noneducational; that is, it is a for-profit business concern. The adult education function in this environment is only viable as long as members of the parent organization see it as contributing to the parent organization's mission.

Schroeder's classification system helps us to identify the relationship between the adult education function and the parent organization. This relationship determines the type and extent of support adult education receives from the parent organization. One of the key issues raised by this system is how central to the mission of the parent organization is the adult and community education function. The answer is often tied directly to how well the organization is doing from a financial standpoint.

Funding Patterns

Apps (1989) developed a framework that identifies one of the most important questions that can be asked: Who pays the bills? In his attempt to describe different funding patterns, Apps identified four primary sources of financial support. The first category of financing is fully or partially tax-supported institutions. Examples of adult and community education organizations in this area include public schools, four- and two-year public colleges and universities, the cooperative extension, and many libraries and museums.

The second category is nonprofit, self-supporting agencies and institutions. Examples include religious organizations; some community-based agencies such as the YMCA, YWCA, and Red Cross; many service clubs such as the Kiwanis; voluntary associations such as the League of Women Voters; professional associations; and worker education programs.

The third category is made up of for-profit providers of adult and community education. Examples of these types of organizations are correspondence schools; proprietary schools; private tutors; private, for-profit colleges and universities; consultants offering adult education programs; how-to books, videos and tapes; computer educational software companies; and educational programs sponsored by business and industry.

The last category is nonorganized learning opportunities. This category includes learning through television and other mass media (apart from courses offered by institutions), the work setting, family, travel, and leisure and recreational activities. Learning in this category is not accomplished through the use of educational programs sponsored by formal organizations.

The value of asking "Who pays?" is that it helps to identify to whom the members of the organization have their primary obligation. In effect, it serves a similar function to Blau and Scott's (1962) question: Who benefits? Asking who pays focuses our attention on whose agenda is paramount and how issues of competing agendas should be resolved.

CATEGORIZING COMMUNITY EDUCATION ORGANIZATIONS

It is problematic to distinguish community education from adult education as fields of practice (Hamilton & Cunningham,

1989) and as fields of inquiry (Dean, 1993b, 1994a). The overlap and confusion are certainly understandable, given the political and economic nature of these fields. Often there is a capri-
cious use of terms; a program in one location is adult education,
while a similar program in another location is community education. Often the name is determined by the funding source.

Despite their similarities, Dean (1993b) identified four criteria that distinguish community education from adult education:

1. In community education, community serves as the context
   for the learning activity.

2. The goals of community education are to improve the quality of life for community members as well as to enhance the
   community as a whole.

3. Education is seen as a process to accomplish these goals as
   well as an outcome of the process (that is, people in the community use educational programs to become more educated).

4. Education is a primary means of achieving goals for improving quality of life in the community.

The last point is important as it distinguishes community education from other forms of civic action, such as political move-
ments, which may use education as a method but not as their
primary or only method of achieving their goals.

Dean (1993b) developed a matrix for understanding the
dynamics of control and impact of community education. The
horizontal dimension is seen as a continuum from local control
of the community education process to remote control, while
the vertical dimension is a continuum from narrow impact of
the community education process in the community to broad
impact (see Figure 2.2).

As the matrix suggests, four types of community education
organizations can be identified. The first quadrant of the matrix
(Type 1) contains community education organizations that are
locally controlled and have broad-based impact in the community. This quadrant includes classic examples of community de-

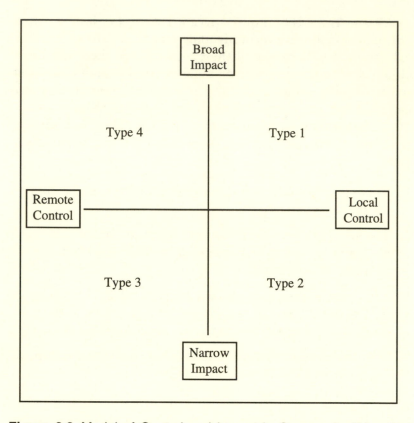

Figure 2.2 Model of Control and Impact in Community Education (Dean, 1993b)

velopment as defined by Biddle and Biddle (1965) or described in the Antigonish movement. The second quadrant (Type 2) includes more specialized community education activities under local control such as community-based adult education organizations, service clubs, voluntary organizations, libraries, and museums. The Type 3 quadrant includes organizations that are not controlled locally but have a specific impact in the community, such as Head Start programs. While many Head Start programs have local advisory boards, the funding and regulations for operations are provided and enforced by the federal government. The result is that a significant portion of the decision making in the organization is out of the hands of the people involved at the local level. The fourth quadrant (Type 4) includes remotely controlled community education that has a broad impact in the community. A good example is the use of mass media to improve the quality of life in a community, such as the smoking cessation and seat belt campaigns of recent years.

The value of the community education matrix is that it can help people understand the dynamics of control and impact as related to decision making in the organization. Pertinent questions to ask include: How are decisions made? How many people are involved? What is the nature of the impact in the community? What is the basis of support in the community for the community education activity?

Dean and Dowling (1987) identified three types of outcomes from community education and development activities: people-related outcomes, organizational outcomes, and programmatic outcomes. People-related outcomes refer to what is learned by the people involved in community education, whether they be organizers or clients. Organizational outcomes refer to the development, maintenance, enhancement, and impact of the actual organization through which the community education activity occurs. Programmatic outcomes refer to the actual educational goals such as career training, basic education, or neighborhood improvement.

McKnight (1995) offers a different view of community education. From her research on community-based, grassroots initiatives, she identified five types of organizations, each offering a different perspective on how learning in community education occurs. All of McKnight's types of community education are altruistic; that is, they describe community education organizations attempting to make a positive impact through peaceful social change. The five types of organizations she identified are self-advocacy groups, both general and focused neighborly affection groups, common good initiatives, and grassroots self-help groups.

Self-advocacy groups are those formed because a small group of people want to right a wrong or address a social injustice. Examples of self-advocacy groups include citizens action groups opposed to landfills or nuclear waste sites. They are characterized by a sense of mission, often even of confrontation in their attempts to reach their goals. Members of self-advocacy groups are motivated by a combination of their own self-interests and their perceived good of the community.

Two types of neighborly affection groups—general and focused—were identified. Neighborly affection is the desire to help others who are less fortunate than those doing the helping. The motivation is often based on the Christian (or other religious) principle of "help your neighbor." General neighborly affection describes groups that address the needs of a geographic area. Often these initiatives are the result of a person or small group who see the need to help others in a geographic area, a neighborhood, or community, where a broad range of issues needs to be addressed. Focused neighborly affection is when the energies of the helpers are focused on a particular need of the less fortunate, for example, creating a playground, developing a health care facility, or providing other specialized services. Often, focused neighborly affection initiatives are the result of a single person who perceives a need and acts to fill that need.

Common good efforts are formed to meet the needs of a broad cross-section of the community. They are formed by representatives of various agencies and organizations who have interests in the targeted community. Often the people represent both their personal interests and those of their employers (such as welfare agencies, hospitals, and universities), which can create conflict for them when their personal assessment of the need is different from their employer's position on the issue. Common good initiatives can be described as collaboratives among established agencies.

Grassroots self-help groups are formed by people with similar needs. For example, a group of senior citizens may get together to meet their needs for companionship and socializing. Grassroots groups often rely on the efforts of a single person or small core group and are usually independent of formal organizations, except for logistical support such as meeting space.

The important distinctions among the community education organizations in McKnight's typology are discerned by asking, Who formed the group, why was it formed, and how will its members go about accomplishing their goals? Groups formed to help the members will be different from those formed to help others. Also, groups formed out of confrontation will operate differently from those formed to serve the needs of others. These are some of the factors to take into account when working with community grassroots organizations.

MAKING DECISIONS TO
IDENTIFY FUTURE DIRECTIONS

Once the assessment of both internal and external factors has been completed, the next step in strategic planning is to integrate the information acquired and attempt to create a comprehensive picture of the organization. The new directions derived from the information obtained may include developing a new mission or vision statement, implementing additional programming, enhancing marketing and public relations, restructuring the organization, or providing additional opportunities for professional development.

An important element of this decision making is to ensure buy-in from all members of the organization. First, the process should be made public; that is, the decisions should be made through the same structure that was used to conduct the rest of the strategic planning. If committees have been used, then the original committee structure should continue to be used, even though new committees may be formed for different stages of the process. If the organization has acted as a committee of the whole to conduct internal and external assessments, then it should continue to act as a committee of the whole.

Open communication and a sense of belonging are critical to success. It is easy for those not agreeing with the decisions derived from strategic planning to claim they were not adequately represented in the process. It is also important not to rush through this stage. There is bound to be more than one interpretation of the information collected during the assessment phase. The various interpretations need to be heard and discussed openly to enhance the sense of community rather than strengthen perceived divisions within the organization.

IMPLEMENTING AND ASSESSING THE PLAN

This stage involves putting into action the decisions reached during strategic planning. It also requires assessing the progress in implementing the plan to determine whether the desired outcomes are being achieved. Usually there will be dates set for the implementation of specific activities or the achievement of certain goals. Results and feedback provide important information for revising, enhancing, and redirecting future strategic planning efforts.

It needs to be reiterated at this point that strategic planning is not a one-time event that constitutes "extra work" for everyone and "is a relief to have over." It needs to become part of the daily operation of the organization so there is a constant cycle of assessment, decision making, and planning.

ANALYZING THE DYNAMICS
IN AN ORGANIZATION

Based on the foregoing discussion, the following questions will help identify the basic organizational structure and the dynamics underlying how an organization works. Each question is presented with some discussion to help readers apply it to understanding their organizations.

• What is the primary purpose of our organization and who is the primary beneficiary? This question is based on Blau and Scott's (1962) analysis of who benefits. This may actually comprise several questions which should be addressed: Has the primary beneficiary been adequately identified? Do we know who we are supposed to be serving? Are we really meeting the needs of our primary beneficiary? How can we better meet the needs of our primary beneficiary? Do we serve multiple primary beneficiaries? Can we effectively serve multiple primary beneficiaries?

- What is the relationship of our organization to its parent organization? This question is based on Schroeder's (1970) typology of adult education organizations. Questions to ask regarding the relationship may include the following: How central to the mission of the parent organization are we? How expendable are we in times of crisis? How can our relationship with the parent organization be strengthened? How can leadership in the parent organization be made to see us as more central to the parent organization's mission?

- What is our current source of financial support? This question is based on Apps's (1989) typology of funding sources. Some possible questions to ask include: How can we strengthen our funding sources? Can we diversify our funding sources? How can we improve our relationship with our funding sources?

- How does our organization function from a rational systems perspective (based on Scott, 1981)? Using the organizational chart in Figure 2.1, draw a diagram of the organization and try to define each position in the chart. Does this activity suggest ways in which the organization can be redesigned to function more smoothly? Are there weak areas where additional support or personnel should be allocated? Are there areas of overlap that could use clarification?

- How does our organization function from a natural systems perspective (based on Scott, 1981)? Is there general agreement among the organization's personnel about the purpose and mission of the organization? Do members of the organization work together or do they pursue divergent goals? Is there a culture in our organization that influences our behavior on the job?

- How does our organization function from a open systems perspective (based on Scott, 1981)? What is the environment in which our organization exists? What is our relationship with our founders and resource providers? What is our relationship with other organizations providing similar or overlapping services? How does our organization fit into the community in which it is located?

SUMMARY

Strategic planning is not a one-time event. In fact, to be effective as a management tool it has to be incorporated into the way the organization functions on a daily basis. Strategic planning should be part of the culture, of the way people solve problems in their jobs, and of how they think about the organization as a whole. If the assessment of internal strengths and weaknesses, external hurdles and opportunities, and decision making is ongoing, then the organization will be prepared to meet the challenges of the future.

The three activities presented at the end of this chapter can help in this process. In Activity 2.1, The Perfect Adult and Community Education Organization, participants will design an organizational structure to achieve a mission statement. This exercise is designed to underscore the idea that any given mission statement or organizational purpose can be reached by different routes. It will also help to form teams and communicate expectations as participants develop the organization to achieve the mission statement of the "picture perfect" organization.

Activity 2.2, Help, Inc.: A Case Study of Changing Times and Values, is an exercise that stresses the importance of understanding organizational culture. The setting is a service agency that has grown significantly over the years and is now experiencing "growing pains." Participants should be able to identify the organizational cultural issues influencing the behavior of the members of the organization.

Activity 2.3, Westville, U.S.A., depicts strategic planning on a community basis. Participants assess the strengths and weaknesses of the community and use the information to address how the community can be improved. All the elements of strategic planning are involved in this activity.

ACTIVITY 2.1
THE PERFECT ADULT AND COMMUNITY EDUCATION ORGANIZATION: UNDERSTANDING MISSION STATEMENTS AND ORGANIZATIONAL STRUCTURE

I. Planning

Goals: Upon completing this activity, participants will be able to identify and discuss the strengths and weaknesses of various organizational designs and the uses and importance of mission statements in organizations.

Materials: Copies of the Perfect Adult and Community Education Organization's mission statement.

Time: 45 minutes to 1 hour.

Size of Group: 10 to 20 people divided into teams of 3 to 5 people each.

Note: It is helpful to define the community which the Perfect Adult and Community Education Organization will serve for the participants. Usually it is best to use the metropolitan area or the county in which the participants reside as the community for this exercise. The exercise can be made more complex by asking each team to develop a budget, marketing campaign, and specific service delivery systems to accomplish various components of the mission statement. Teams can also write mission statements for various subunits within their organization. Also, while the teams are developing their plans, the facilitator should resist commenting on the organizational structure of the teams. To do so may influence how the participants design their organizations. This activity works best when the various teams develop different approaches to accomplishing the mission statement.

II. Involvement

Step 1: Present the concept of organizational structure to participants. This can be done by having participants read Chapter 2 in this book, or by presenting them with a brief lecture. (Note: The lecture will add time to the activity.)

Step 2: Ask participants to move into teams of three to five people each, and provide each team with a copy of the mission statement.

Step 3: Tell the teams they have 30 minutes to develop an organizational structure that will meet the goals of the mission statement. Indicate that one person from each team can be chosen to present the team's organizational plan, or that the entire team may make a group presentation.

Step 4: When all teams have completed the exercise, ask for volunteers to present the team's plan. After all of the plans have been discussed, generate discussion about the strengths and weaknesses of the various plans.

III. Reflection, Generalization, and Application

The debriefing should include a discussion of the organizational structures presented by each team. It should, of course, be pointed out that there is no such thing as a "perfect" organization. The organizational structures developed by the teams should be compared to the literature (as presented in Chapter 2) and various organizations with which the participants are familiar. This will enable them to identify and discuss the strengths and weaknesses of each plan realistically and in more detail. Issues which can be discussed include vertical versus horizontal organizational structure, effectiveness of service delivery systems, use of and/or collaboration with existing agencies, use of volunteers, degree of bureaucracy, and ties to community-based groups.

IV. Follow-up

As a follow-up activity, have participants take a critical look at the organizational structure of the organization(s) in which they currently work. They may then be able to make suggestions for improving the structure and service delivery systems.

V. Activity

The mission statement should be provided to each team. You may photocopy it or write the information on a transparency overhead or chalkboard.

THE PERFECT ADULT AND COMMUNITY EDUCATION ORGANIZATION MISSION STATEMENT

The purpose of this organization is to improve the quality of life in the community by providing better access to health services, employment, housing, and education for all members of the community.

The Task

Your task is to develop an organizational plan to achieve the objective presented in the mission statement. The team has generous resources and support to accomplish the mission. Your plan should include all full- and part-time positions, offices, collaboration with other organizations, and relationships to various constituencies in the community.

ACTIVITY 2.2
HELP, INC.: A CASE STUDY OF
CHANGING TIMES AND VALUES

I. Planning

Goals: After completing this case study, learners will be able to identify the elements of organizational culture and their influences on the behavior of members of the organization.
Materials: Copies of the case study for each participant.
Time: Approximately 1 hour.
Size of Group: Works best with small groups of 3 to 6 people.

II. Involvement

Directions: Have participants review Chapter 2, Implementing Strategic Planning, prior to the case study. Have participants read the case study individually and then in small groups of three to six, discuss the questions at the end of the case study. A discussion among the small groups may be added to identify as many differences of opinion as possible.

III. Reflection, Generalization, and Application

Discussion of the case study should focus on the elements of organizational culture according to the definition of Schein (1985) which can be identified in the case. Discussion of the culture conflict should flow from the identification of the nature of the culture in the organization. It should be noted that organizational culture is an extremely complex and subtle phenomenon and that only fragments of it can be noted from a short case study such as this.

IV. Follow-up

Concepts learned from the case study can be applied to the organization in which the participants work by having them complete an analysis of their own organization using Schein's definitions and the other information provided in Chapter 2.

V. Activity

This activity may be duplicated so that each participant will have a copy.

HELP, INC.:
A CASE STUDY OF CHANGING TIMES AND VALUES

Help, Inc. was founded in 1967 when a local pastor, Reverend Smith, decided to follow through on his threat to "do something about poverty and hopelessness" in his city. The organization was founded with the determination of Rev. Smith and several small grants from area churches. Since that time, Help, Inc. has grown to an organization of 23 employees and is now funded from a variety of sources including churches, United Way, private foundations, and local government money. The organization primarily provides services to residents of several communities on the east and south sides of the city; these are lower income, high crime areas, and in some cases, neighborhoods with aging residents. Among the many problems faced are unemployment, lower-income single-parent families, absentee landlords, drug abuse, gang presence and in some cases violence, lack of proper recreational activities, and a general feeling of hopelessness on the part of many residents.

For over 30 years, Help, Inc. has been providing services

such as family counseling, job development and referral, and recreational programs. In addition, Help, Inc. has worked closely with a variety of other community and governmental agencies to provide referral and coordination of services. In the past 10 years, Help, Inc. has offered adult basic education and literacy classes in conjunction with the public library.

The Rev. Smith is a unique character. He possesses a strong sense of right and wrong. He believes, quite unconditionally, that there is only one way to accomplish the mission of Help, Inc. That is to go out each day and help at least one person. He is fond of saying, "Do one good thing each day, and you can help a lot of people in your lifetime." The mission statement for Help, Inc. reflects the reverend's philosophy:

> The employees, friends, and supporters of Help, Inc. are dedicated to making our community a better place to live by helping people cope with their problems so that they can grow, be strong, and in turn help others. In this way, we will overcome the ills of poverty, racism, unemployment, and hopelessness so our children will have a better place to live and a better life.

Recent changes in the community have forced some community members to speak out about the conditions. One such person is Victoria Johnson. She has led a movement to make city government more responsive to community needs by addressing the issues of high unemployment rates, drug abuse, and gang violence. Her particular issue, however, has been the plight of the older members of the community who live in fear and sometimes in poverty. Ms. Johnson has had the ear of Rev. Smith who is concerned about the same issues. Ms. Johnson has been able to get the attention of the press on the social conditions in her community. The result is that the city and county government are now trying to "act concerned" but have not yet taken concrete action. While Ms. Johnson and Rev. Smith have been friends for years, she is now publicly beginning to question the effectiveness of Help, Inc. to intervene in the issues.

Mary Simpson, coordinator of family counseling, is one of six employees who have been with Help, Inc. since the early days. Mary and her colleagues are called the "old-timers" by the others. Mary Simpson has always acted as Rev. Smith's second in command and has traditionally run the agency when he was out on one of his frequent fund-raising campaigns. Melissa Strong is the secretary, and a friend of Rev Smith. She has been with Help, Inc. since its inception. She provides the type of steady, reliable day-to-day service the agency needs to function. Sam Williams, coordinator of recreational programs, started at Help, Inc. just three years after Mary Simpson. He has developed a reputation in the community as someone who cares and has become a favorite of the youth in the city.

In the early days, the staff of a half-dozen or so employees worked as an informal team without clear lines of authority or responsibility. They all functioned as family counselors, tutors, and even bus drivers when necessary. There was a feeling of "we are all in this together and each of us will do whatever is necessary to get the job done." Since 1990 the staff has more than doubled from 10 to the present 23 employees. Most of the new positions are the result of increased funding from the city and several new grants, including a grant to provide ABE and literacy instruction. Presently, Help, Inc. has four divisions, each with a coordinator: Mary Simpson is coordinator of family counseling with 5 counselors working under her direction; Sam Williams is coordinator of recreational programs and supervises 7 part-time recreational specialists working at various schools and centers around the city; Sandra Lewis is coordinator of educational services and has 3 tutors and 17 volunteers working for her; and Sally Allan, coordinator of Help, Inc. Homeless Shelter, supervises 2 employees.

Sandra Lewis was hired in 1991 as coordinator of educational services to oversee the literacy and ABE programs. A dedicated adult educator, Sandra was attracted to Help, Inc. because she saw potential for the agency to expand its educational programs to include vocational training. She believed she was the person who could lead such an expansion. Ralph Topper was hired as a family caseworker in 1989. Although relatively new to the organization and only a mediocre counselor, he has already made his mark by redesigning the record-keeping system in the office to be computer-based. In addition, he has written three grants for more than $100,000 in the past five years. Sandra, Ralph, and many of the other people hired after 1990 are often referred to as the "new guard."

Ralph and Sandra developed a plan to further expand Help, Inc. by seeking funding for federal retraining programs and then linking the agency with the area vocational-technical school. The linkage, if successful, could bring in lots of new money for Help, Inc., but would require the agency to be responsible to the school board and the county commissioners (for JTPA funds). Both the school board and the county commissioners have a reputation for being very meddlesome in the affairs of their subcontractors. Ralph believes that this is a small price to pay for the drastic increase in revenues and the ability to provide new services.

Mary Simpson has come out publicly against the plan, stating that the loss of autonomy for Help, Inc. would undermine its ability to serve the community. She reminds the employees every chance she gets that the success of Help, Inc. comes from its credibility in the community. She cites the presence of Victoria Johnson as an example. Mary worries that coming under the control of the school board and the county will make Help, Inc. even less responsive to the concerns of Ms. Johnson than it is now. She is very concerned that the proposed changes will ultimately negate all of the work she, Sam Williams, Rev. Smith, and the other old-timers have accomplished over the years.

The Advisory Board of Help, Inc. is an interesting mix of socially concerned people and social climbers. Over the years a balance between the board's functions and Rev. Smith's domain has been established. The board is kept informed but does not get involved unless major changes in policy or personnel are involved. This position is exemplified by James Long, president and member of the board since Help, Inc. started. He is a strong supporter of Rev. Smith and the hands-off approach the board has taken over the years. Samantha Stewart, a newer member of the board, on the other hand, has become concerned over the lack of accountability of funds in Help, Inc. and has recently made a proposal that the books of the agency be audited. She has been on the board for three years and is the wife of a local bank president. The other 10 members of the board are fairly equally divided between supporting the position of James Long and that of Samantha Stewart.

Trouble between the old-timers and the new guard has been brewing for some time. It came to a head at a general staff meeting when Rev. Smith unexpectedly announced his retirement, citing health as the reason. At the meeting he gave no clue as to who he would recommend as his successor. Unfortunately, his health became critical a few days after the meeting and now it looks like he will not be able to name a successor. As might be expected, the rumor mill started going full tilt with older employees favoring Mary Simpson while newer employees tended to favor Ralph Topper. Each of these people wants to assume leadership. Mary feels she deserves it because she has over 25 years of service with Help, Inc. In addition, she cites the strong reputation she has in the community and her adherence to the original mission of the agency as well as the philosophy of Rev. Smith. Ralph's case rests with his updated knowledge of computers, office management, and his demonstrated ability to get grants. The board will decide at its next meeting. Both Ralph and Mary have applied for the position.

Discussion Questions

1. What are the issues between the "old-timers" and the "new guard"?

2. How do these issues reflect the espoused values and basic assumptions of the two groups?

3. Is the original mission and philosophy of Rev. Smith still viable? If so, how should it be carried out? If not, how should it be changed?

4. Which person do you feel is best suited to assume leadership of Help, Inc.?

ACTIVITY 2.3
WESTVILLE, U.S.A.: A CASE STUDY
IN COMMUNITY EDUCATION

I. Planning

Goals: Upon completing this activity, participants will be able to conduct a community-wide needs assessment, understand the dynamics of a town hall meeting, identify a variety of important roles within the community, and understand the dynamics of community education development.

Materials: The Westville, U.S.A., case study, pencils and paper for discussion and notes, and creative imaginations.

Time: 1 to 2 hours.

Size of Group: 10 to 25 participants.

II. Involvement

Step 1. Have the participants carefully read over the case study, noting the locations of the river, various schools, parks, the university, key industrial areas, and shopping locations on the Westville map.

Step 2. Have the group analyze and discuss the strengths, limitations, special needs, and resources available for Westville. The questions at the end of the case study are provided for this purpose.

Step 3. Have the group participate in a Westville town hall meeting using various roles provided at the end of the case study. Each participant should assume a role and participate in the town meeting. The agenda of the town meeting is to (1) identify the needs of Westville, (2) creation a vision and mission statement for Westville, and (3) develop a community education program that makes use of the schools and establishes an empowering process for neighborhoods in which community problems are addressed.

III. Reflection and Generalization

The group, through role playing and experiencing a town hall meeting, practices community assessment by identifying key problems that the "divided" Westville is experiencing, discusses the resources available to the town, and considers the possibility of establishing a community education program to address some of the major problems and issues related to the Westville community.

IV. Application and Follow-up

Participants should be able to transfer learning from this case study to a variety of situations including conducting assessment activities, participating in town hall meetings, participating in various leadership and supportive roles, undergoing and resolving conflicts, developing community education programs as a vehicle for empowering the community, and getting people involved in the process.

V. Activity

This activity may be reproduced for the participants.

WESTVILLE, U.S.A.: A CASE STUDY IN COMMUNITY EDUCATION

Westville, which is located in the Midwest, has a population of approximately 71,000 people. The usual diversified industries and numerous small companies employ the work force. Although the town has the cyclical employment problems of many communities, a strike in any one industry would not paralyze the city. In the event of a layoff or labor problems, the affected workers are sometimes able to find temporary employment, although at a reduced income. The unemployment level has been around 7 percent in the past few years. Typically those who are unemployed lack work skills and significant work experience; the majority of the unemployed are minorities.

The community has grown rapidly since the 1960 census which showed 25,000 people. Then, 100 percent of the population was white, and in the 1970 census when the population grew to 50,000 there were only about 150 nonwhite or minority families. Current statistics reveal approximately 12 percent of the population are minorities. Income in Westville ranges from less than $7,000 to over $175,000 per family with about 7 percent considered to be earning below the poverty line.

Although the community has been rapidly expanding, it has the problem of deterioration in its original business district or city center area. This area and the surrounding residential area are occupied, in large part, by the city's minority population. The whole city center area is suffering from decreasing property values due to rezoning for multiple dwellings and the influx of lower economic class white and minority families. Many long-established businesses have moved to the new shopping centers near the northeast and northwest city limits. Incidents of arson and robberies are on the increase in the city center or downtown area, and the welfare rolls are expanding.

In addition to the downtown shopping district, the city has two other large shopping centers which lie on the edge of the city. These have attracted much of the former downtown businesses so that most people in the community seldom visit the older sections of Westville. Business in the community is much the same as in other cities of similar size. There are the usual array of goods and services available. In addition to serving urban needs, Westville is the marketing and purchasing center for farmers within a 30 to 40 mile radius. An increasing number of retail stores remain open at night and on weekends to accommodate the buying public.

A survey showed that 66 percent of the populace in Westville claim to be Protestant, 24 percent claim they are Catholic, and 10 percent claim "other" or no religious affiliation. Of the Protestants there are no particularly predominant denominations although there are a high percentage who claim to be either Methodists or Baptists. The Catholics provide parochial education for most of their elementary age children. The churches advocate good works, of course, so long as "we don't rock the boat!"

A few cultural opportunities have been developed in Westville. The usual women's clubs, sororities, and church groups provide "culture" and "support" to the citizens of the community. A public library and its three branch libraries serve the community. At present, there is no large civic auditorium (a high school auditorium is used), but there are plans to build one soon which will be financed through community donations and local support.

There are eight recreation areas used as community parks. Two are located in the downtown area. The Parks and Recreation Department has spend a large part of its time and funds to beautify Westville. Several park sites have been purchased on the fringes of the city, but they are only "appreciated" there. Recreation is largely available through "private" swimming pools and bathing clubs. Many teenagers claim there is nothing to do in Westville.

Currently, the city has two senior high schools, two middle schools, eight elementary schools and one parochial school (kindergarten through the eighth grade). The older center-city schools are overcrowded, but no plans are being formulated to alleviate the situation. The curriculum in the schools has remained traditional; however, one elementary school is attempting a nongraded curriculum for the first time this year. The older schools, which include the Main Street High School and one of the middle schools, are both antiquated. The school system does offer adult education and community enrichment classes at night, but little effort is being made to publicize them. The attendance at these programs is light. A few classes are offered for those who want to complete their high school training or GED. They are held in the new high school if there are enough students to make up a class. Attempts are being made to approve construction of a building for vocational education—a situation which developed after the federal government informed the local school board that it would furnish half of the money. Lack of money always seems to be the big problem as far as the Westville school board is concerned. In addition to the public and parochial schools in Westville, there is a medium-size state university which serves about 18,000 students and a commercial school called the Midwest Business College.

Westville has many service organizations: Lions Club, Optimist Club, Rotary, Kiwanis, etc., as well as the usual service agencies. These include a branch of employment security, welfare, the Salvation Army, the United Way, YMCA, YWCA, Boys/Girls Club, the American Cancer Society, Urban League, Community Action Council, Family Services, Goodwill Industries, the Comprehensive Mental Health Association, and others.

There use to be two separate newspapers, a morning and evening paper, each operated by people with "opposite" political views. They were operated out of the same building, but very recently, the newspapers merged into one daily paper. There are three local radio stations and a public television station. There is a major regional teaching hospital in the area serving the health care needs of Westville.

Westville citizens, rather conservative by nature, are mostly content to leave matters as they are. According to Chamber of Commerce records, nothing has been done in the past 50 years to upset any long-established city policies. However, a group of local citizens has recently formed a Council of Action Committee spearheaded by the local Jaycees to attempt to move Westville off "dead center."

Westville is divided geographically, politically, racially, and economically by the river that flows through the center of the town. North and west sections of Westville are inhabited by the wealthy Republican conservative citizens who live around the state university area. The south and east areas are inhabited by the poorer Democratic minorities and the poor white transplants from the south who live near the industrial centers where there is a higher level of crime and drugs. The construction of homes is taking place at a rapid rate in the northwest area. Local real estate brokers have successfully kept Westville somewhat segregated through redefining and redistricting strategies, but open housing is being passionately debated at the Westville Council meetings. At present, however, the procedures are moving rather slowly yet steadily. Everyone is optimistic that a solution will be found.

Assessment of Westville, U.S.A.

1. List and describe the strengths and limitations of Westville.
2. Describe the existing (physical, material, and personnel) resources available for Westville.
3. Diagnose what you believe are the special Westville needs and existing community problems.
4. Recommend ways to meet the needs and solve the problems.
5. Discuss how you might use interagency and collaborative strategies for assisting Westville to solve its problems.
6. List three or more strategies for establishing a visioning process for community education development for Westville.
7. Describe some of the programmatic effects, outcomes, and consequences for Westville.
8. Describe how you would evaluate your effectiveness as a

Westville community educator and/or as an advocate for change.

9. Offer additional comments or suggestions.

Roles for the Westville Town Hall Meeting

1. Mayor
2. Superintendent of schools
3. Lawyer
4. Industrialist
5. Militant leader of poor and less privileged
6. Farmer
7. Teenage youth
8. President of the Jaycees
9. Businessman
10. President of the PTA Council
11. Minister
12. Senior citizen
13. Labor leader
14. Hospital administrator
15. Inner city mother
16. Suburban white professional
17. City councilperson
18. Director of city recreation
19. Building contractor or real estate broker
20. City engineer
21. College student
22. Teacher
23. City planner
24. Member of news media
25. Other community members

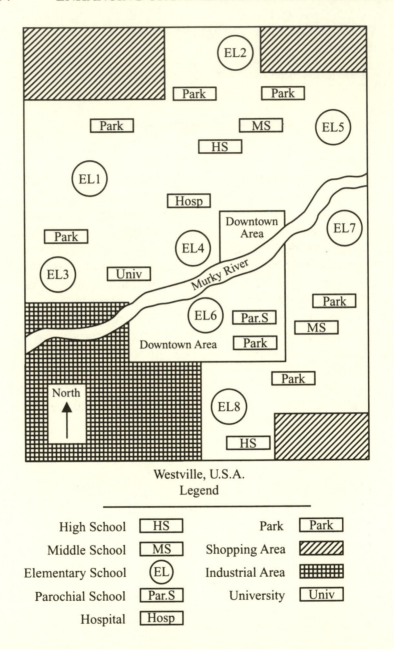

Westville, U.S.A.
Legend

High School	HS	Park	Park
Middle School	MS	Shopping Area	
Elementary School	EL	Industrial Area	
Parochial School	Par.S	University	Univ
Hospital	Hosp		

CHAPTER 3

Writing Grant Proposals and Securing Funds

Acquiring adequate funding is one of the most critical challenges facing many adult and community education organizations. Without adequate funding, most agencies would not be able to continue operating or would function at a far less effective level. Finding new sources of funding is an ongoing challenge for many organizations. Grant research and proposal writing can mean the difference between a healthy organization and one that is just keeping its head above water. Before an organization can secure grants or other forms of funding, it must first conduct thorough research into the types of funding available. By identifying sources, grant options, and potential sponsors, the organization can begin the process of turning an idea into a reality.

IDEA DEVELOPMENT

The key to a successful proposal is coming up with a realistic idea for improvement. An idea that has been thoughtfully assessed, in terms of feasibility and current literature in the field, provides the basis to formulate activities that can be matched with and by funding source(s) and sponsors who are interested in developing partnerships and funding activities. A well-defined and conceptualized idea or plan allows for all of the subsequent proposal development steps to occur. Free-form thinking, brainstorming, and wish lists are several ways to generate ideas and discussion.

Financial support for project activities can come from a diverse range of sources. The more traditional requests for funding include research projects, instructional improvement, social services, welfare, and medical projects. In addition, operating costs and special projects in the arts and humanities, such as funds for planning and development purposes, may be used.

A STEP-BY-STEP APPROACH

Once an idea has been chosen, it is time to develop an outline for the proposal. The outline reveals pertinent data and information, as well as any hidden needs, shortfalls, or issues. It should be brief and realistic while answering the following conceptual questions.

1. What is the name of the project?

2. Who will be involved? (List names, titles, credentials, qualifications, and experience.)

3. Where will the project be located? (Note special facilities provided.)

4. When should the project begin and end? (Include management plan and timeline.)

5. Why do the project? (Provide mission statement, needs analysis, and rationale.)

6. What is expected to be accomplished by the project? (State goals and objectives as well as special activities.)

7. How will the project be accomplished? (Describe methods and procedures.)

8. Why are you and your organization qualified to do the project? (Indicate qualified personnel and offer letters of support.)

9. How will the results be measured, evaluated, and distributed? (Describe evaluation and dissemination of results.)

10. How much will the project cost? (Estimate direct and indirect costs through an effective budget and explanation of expenses.)

Answering these questions will provide an outline and conceptual framework for the grant writing process, as well as ensuring the project is feasible, doable, and necessary. In Activity 3.1, EDCILL Grant Writing Simulation, readers will have the opportunity to develop a grant proposal in response to a mock RFP based on an actual federal format.

FUNDING SOURCES

According to Lowry (1995), the search for funding sources should begin while the idea for the proposal is being developed. To succeed in obtaining financial support, the relationship between the project activities and the interests of the funding sponsor must be clearly communicated and linked. However, the specific activities defined for any idea may be shaped somewhat by the specific interests of potential sponsors. Three topics are addressed in this section. First, the identification of funding sources is discussed. Second, types of funding sources are discussed. Third, some print, computer, and electronic directories for information on grant money are listed.

Identification of Funding Sources

Finding the most appropriate source of funding for a project is an important and time-consuming activity. Organizations are fortunate that have an office or person responsible for maintaining a grant library, monitoring grant information sources, and providing assistance for identification of potential sources of support. If, however, sources must be identified without assistance, three questions may serve as guidelines in the search:

1. What are the available sources of funding?

2. Where can information on the funding organization be obtained?

3. What specific information is needed for a proposed project?

When seeking support for any project, all potential sources should be considered. Locating the sources of funds is a vital step in becoming a successful grant seeker.

Types of Funding Sources

Financial assistance can come from a variety of sources. The federal government provides by far the largest portion of support, while foundations provide substantially less but significant amounts. The remaining sources account for a small part of the total funds dispersed annually. Typical funding sources include:

- government sources (federal, state, regional/county)
- private foundations (family, corporate, and community)
- private businesses (corporations and industries, universities, libraries, museums, and professional associations)
- philanthropic individuals and special financial groups

Whatever funding source is sought or used, grants are not made to individuals but to agencies which are nonprofit and tax exempt; that is, those that have a 501(c)(3) nonprofit status. Funding sources want to be assured that there is a designated qualified agent overseeing and controlling the expenditures of grant funds. Secondly, foundations and corporate-giving sources need to maintain their own tax-exempt 501(c)(3) or 509 status with the Internal Revenue Service; therefore, they must only award grants to nonprofit agencies and organizations.

Federal Agencies

Generally, federal agencies have the most accessible information and are considered the most viable source of funding. Grant programs often originate from legislation that is in response to critical social and health needs, such as AIDS studies, cancer research, or major health and educational issues (see the Federal Register). Timelines for securing grants are usually shorter than for other funding sources, but proposals for funds are driven by the federal funding cycle. In addition, proposals for federal grants often require following complex guidelines, including restrictions and strict reporting procedures. Limited entitlement funds and federal proposals also involve a more detailed review process, resulting in only the most effective proposals gaining funding.

State Agencies

Many of the major funds from state agencies are granted to state authorities from federal government offices. There is less intense competition when applying for funds through state agencies than from the federal sources; however, rigid state guidelines, restrictions, and reporting procedures often apply.

Private Foundations

There are approximately 30,000 foundations in the United States which award $8 billion annually to volunteer and not-for-profit organizations. Typically, there are three private sources from which to secure grant monies.

Family foundation assets come from family bequests to be used for purposes that are important to the donors. Grants are usually limited to specific purposes and/or particular geographic or regional locations.

Corporate funds (*a corpus*) are started and maintained through profits from companies and are used for purposes determined by the parent corporation. Funds are usually for products, services, and technical assistance.

Community foundation assets come from donors within the community and are designed specifically for projects that will benefit or enhance the community. Usually, the grants are limited in scope, geography, or financial support.

Private Businesses

Businesses often have no established programs or written policy regarding grants and donations; however, this is a good source for contributions. Many companies are interested in projects that will generate quality products, lower costs, satisfied employees, and better public and community sponsored relationships.

Although private businesses typically do not publicize their charitable efforts, many maintain some contribution projects which include grants. They are called corporate giving programs and may be linked to the nature of their businesses. For example, IBM fosters a strong interest in computer education, and the 3-M Company is interested in supporting programs in engineering, mining, and metallurgy.

Philanthropic Individuals and Special Financial Groups

The last funding group includes special projects, personal interests, and restricted donations from the public sector. These usually come in the form of trusts and endowments from individuals in the community. Such philanthropic sources are often difficult to identify. In planning this type of fund-raising, it is vital to be knowledgeable about local funders.

Print, Computer, and Electronic Sources of Funding

Advances in technology have made researching and applying for grants easier. Many granting entities and foundations utilize Requests for Proposals (RFP), often providing guidelines and applications on the Internet. Following are some resources currently available, but new ones are created and introduced every day.

Catalog of Federal Domestic Assistance
The Commerce Business Daily
The Directory of Corporate Philanthropy
The Federal Grants and Contracts Weekly
The Federal Register
The Foundation Directory(ies)
The Foundation Grants Index
The Foundation News
Guide to Department of Educational Administered Programs,
    U.S. Department of Education

Taft Corporate Giving Directory
Taft Foundation Reporter

The following list of computer data bases and electronic sources will help the researcher acquire up-to-date information:

BRS Search Service
CBD ALERT Software
COMPUSERVE, INC.
DIALOG INFORMATION SERVICES
DIALOG, VUTEXT, WILSONLINE
EASYNET
FAPRS (Federal Assistance Program Retrieval System)
GRANTSrequest @ note.GOV)
GRANT$SEARCH The Office of Federal Programs
IQUEST
NEWSNET
NEXIS
NSF GRANTS BULLETIN BOARD INTERNET:
    (grants @ NSF)

PROPOSAL DEVELOPMENT

Proposal development consists of several distinct tasks. First to be considered here are the preliminary steps, which include the things that must be addressed prior to writing the proposal. Second, the letter of inquiry is described. This letter is generally submitted in advance of a proposal. Third, the components of an actual proposal narrative are described. Fourth, the post-application process is examined. Finally, outcomes of the proposal review are identified and discussed.

Preliminary Steps

Before a written statement of a proposed project is constructed, it is important to think through the global aspects of the design. According to Murk (1992) it will be helpful to:

- Identify the needs of the appropriate funding agencies.
- Determine the nature of the project and how it will be conducted.
- Review personnel qualifications.
- Discuss the program needs of the project.
- Determine the financial scope and timetable for the project.
- Conduct a literature search to determine perspective and relevancy.
- Check previous award lists for feasibility, accuracy, and appropriateness.

After identifying possible financial sources, it is important to review the overall scope and mission of the funding source, understand the current and emerging interests of the funding source, and reassess the likelihood of funding for the project. For example, the Kellogg Foundation has had a strong interest in funding continuing education and lifelong learning projects over the years. The needs and priorities of funders may change, however, and it is vital to know the current interests of funders. Once that is done, determine where the project fits in the agency's plans and assess the best form of contact with the funding source: that is, letter of inquiry, prospectus, telephone call, or personal visit.

The Letter of Inquiry

After identifying the funding source(s) for the project, the next step is to write a well-organized letter of inquiry (intent) that follows the funding source's specific instructions and protocol procedures. Up front, communicate the agency's needs and why the project is important. Next, establish the credibility and capability of the people who will carry out the project and describe how the project's outcomes will be measured. The most important questions that should be addressed in the letter of inquiry are answered in the outline and subsequent research. (See A Step-by-Step Approach.)

The initial letter of inquiry, or preapplication phase, is presented as one or two typed, single-spaced pages that answer the questions listed previously. Often grant seekers add an optional third page with an estimated budget of expenses.

Other important suggestions include stating a clear, concise purpose for the project. Describe the proposed idea in a positive way and review similar past funded projects. Build in a reasonable set of procedures as a plan for how the project will be managed and evaluated. Describe other sources of funding or "in kind" matching funds. Indicate that the agency is prepared to submit a full proposal and to answer any questions. Remember to use action verbs (for example, to list, to describe, to evaluate, to conclude, or to summarize) and be sure that the amount requested is within the source's guidelines.

The letter should be posted on the agency's letterhead with its tax exempt 501(c)(3) number and should be signed by an authorized person (CEO) or someone (the director) who is willing to implement the proposed project. The letter of inquiry can be followed up by a telephone call or personal visit to the funding source.

Proposal Narrative Components

If a format is specified by the funding source, then follow it precisely. Unless otherwise stated in the funding source's guidelines, a proposal will contain the following components. (See Figure 3.1 for a completed proposal outline.)

I. Cover Sheet

This cover sheet, sometimes referred to as the face sheet or title page, should be the first (unnumbered) page and should contain the following information clearly identified in itemized form. If a title or cover page is provided by the funding source as part of the application process, use that form and complete all requested information. Otherwise, use the guidelines listed below.

A. Name of the funding source

B. Name of the applicant organization or institution

C. Project title

Grant Proposal Outline

Section	Contents
Section I	Cover Sheet—application form(s), assurances.
Section II	Abstract or Executive Summary—usually one page, single spaced, approximately 350 words.
Section III	Applicant organization or institution—including history, structure, experience.
Section IV	Table of Contents.
Section V	Introduction—general overview/mission of the institution including facilities and qualified staff.
Section VI	Problem Statement—including research questions to be addressed, review of community and/or institutional needs, project rationale or purpose of the study, and review of related literature and/or creative local solution to the problems.
Section VII	Goals and Objectives—including general/major goals and objectives, proposal solutions, expected outcomes, and measurable results.
Section VIII	Program Narrative—including procedures, activities specified, strategies, research design, operational format, action/management plan, and timeline of activities.
Section IX	Evaluation—including formative evaluation of procedures and process and summative evaluation of products or outcomes.
Section X	Dissemination—for example, distribution of results, replicability, utilization plan, transferability, recommendations, program benefits, news articles about the program's success, public service announcements about the program, conference presentations, or articles about the program.
Section XI	Facilities—including space requirements and details about housing and equipment (for example, floor plans describing square footage).
Section XII	Personnel—including staff capabilities, special competencies, cooperative arrangements (for example, memoranda of understanding between agencies), and written job descriptions for services included in the proposal.

Section	Contents
Section XIII	Budget—including a budget and narrative that address financial skeleton, outline of expenses, fixed and variable charges, and direct and indirect charges.
Section XIV	Appendixes—for example, background material, 501(c)(3) certificate, annual financial reports, resumes and biographical sketches of personnel, brochures from programs or the institution, letters of support, charts, graphs, and other supportive material such as statistical data/demographic data.

Figure 3.1 An example of a complete grant proposal outline and format

D. Names, titles, telephone numbers, and signatures of project members

E. Mailing address(es) and office phone number(s)

F. Project duration: anticipated start-up date and final date of project

G. Total project dollar amount requested (including indirect costs)

H. Project director's name, title, and signature (or authorized person representing the organization)

I. Federal not-for-profit or 501(c)(3) status number

II. Abstract or Executive Summary

The title and abstract are the first things read in a proposal, so it is imperative that they clearly convey the essence of the project.

Following the cover page, begin the next page with the project title as the centered heading. An abstract of one to three paragraphs in length (250–300 words) and limited to no more than one page should appear. The abstract should be succinct, providing the reviewer with a clear overview of the project, including a statement of need, objectives, methodologies, significant or intended outcomes, and any innovative elements. The abstract should be descriptive, enthusiastic, and written so that the reader will want to read the entire proposal. Following the last paragraph, the total dollar amount requested and the project duration dates should be identified. These may be itemized at the left of the page.

III. Applicant Organization or Institution

A description of the applicant organization or institution should address the following: statement of purpose, brief historic reference, specific strengths, administrative structure pertinent to the proposed project, experience in the administration of externally funded projects, grant and contract income (if appropriate), geographic location (describing how the location will be an asset or critical to the success to the proposed project), and the relationship existing (if any) between the organization, its surrounding community, and/or other similar organizations.

IV. Table of Contents

Limit the table of contents to a single page following the description of the applicant organization or institution. A list of all the major sections of the narrative should be presented. If an outline style is used throughout the narrative, identify each division of the table of contents accordingly. Section identifications should be placed to the left of each major heading; page numbers should be located to the right. Important criteria should be incorporated into headings or subheadings. If there are more than three tables or figures, a list of tables, figures, and/or illustrations should be included. Page references for bibliography, references, and each appendix are included.

V. Introduction

According to Lowry (1995) the most fundable projects either propose a new approach to an old problem or apply an old approach to a new problem. If the subject matter has not been studied or the approach is new, establish the need to explore the topic further or to use a new strategy. Limit the definition of the problem to something that can be realistically addressed.

Provide an overview of the program, institution, and area of study that will capture the attention of the reviewer. Make the introduction a brief summary of the problem, proposed method of solution, and anticipated outcomes. This is also an opportunity to demonstrate how the project or work proposed is unique and interesting.

Reference current literature in the field, previous work, preliminary results, and relevant statistics to support the need. Establish any gaps in the literature that may be addressed by the project. Present the literature review in a positive light and demonstrate the importance of the area of research to the mission and priorities of the funding source. End with two or three sentences about the general purpose or goal of the project. This section should be limited to two or three pages.

VI. Problem Statement

Now is the time to define the problem to be solved or need to be addressed. This should be a succinct analysis, leaving no doubt in the reviewer's mind that a real challenge exists and that funding it is worthwhile. This section should contain documentation to help build a case for funding the project. A well-developed problem statement demonstrates that the need is both logical and deserving of financial support.

VII. Goals and Objectives

Goals are general statements that establish how the problem will be solved or how the project needs will be met. They are necessary to ensure the project is feasible and, once started, remains on track. It is helpful to use the active voice and action verbs, such as prepare, train, and recruit, when preparing goal statements.

Objectives are statements of precise outcomes which can be measured to determine actual accomplishments. They are not methods or means to accomplish goals. Objectives state what the project director and associates intend to accomplish and by when.

The objectives detail how the project will address the problem, need, or gap in knowledge presented in the Introduction section. Present realistic, measurable, time-bound objectives to address each issue identified in the Introduction and Problem Statement sections.

This section should itemize the anticipated outcomes of the study, not what the project director intends to do or the areas to be researched. It should include a brief narrative and a definitive statement such as: "At the completion of this project, the following objectives will have been attained." This can be followed by a listing of specific anticipated results.

State the significance or impact of achieving the objectives. Indicate why the work is important. For example, the project might solve a problem, unveil new knowledge, create a model, or improve a scientific technique. Finally, distinguish clearly between long-range goals and short-range objectives for which funding is being sought.

VIII. Program Narrative

The narrative section contains explicit statements clearly defining the methods by which the problem can be solved. A logical step-by-step procedure should be outlined in a chronological sequence, including a project timetable. Professionally produced diagrams, charts, graphs, maps, and milestone charts can be included where they will aid the reviewer(s).

The program narrative is the place to convince the reviewer that the project personnel, proposed methods, and available facilities provide the best possible conditions for solving the existing problem. The narrative explains how the problem will be solved and what methods will be employed to gather and use the information. Be specific about the program's activities, utilization of personnel, and how data will be compiled.

IX. Evaluation

Increasingly, funding agencies are requesting data in the form of post-project reports that demonstrate the degree to which project objectives are met. This section explains how the success of the project will be measured.

A proposal should include an outline of intended evaluation techniques, including the development of special testing instruments, if necessary, and the conditions under which the evaluation will take place. Quantitative, rather than qualitative, data should be the result. However, it is possible to supply interviews, cases, and ethnographic or qualitative procedures to support the statistics. If subsequent grant requests for the continuation of the project in future years are anticipated, the data collected as a result of this section will be invaluable. It will be instrumental in validating the success of the initial grant, thus reinforcing through documentation any statements that may be in future proposals.

X. Dissemination

Basically this section describes how the outcomes of the proposed idea, together with the conclusions and recommendations, are to be reported. It further lists the benefits/significance of the project to whom and how. It is used to stimulate ideas, suggestions, and constructive criticism from others. The dissemination of results also helps to inform interested groups about the project and to gain additional support from desired groups. Finally, it shares a model for replication.

As the last narrative section of the proposal, this section should be imaginative and forward looking, yet realistic and practical. It is used to inform the funding source how the project director will maximize the impact of the project. Journal publications, books, presentations and other publications are illustrations of good publicity and public relations for the project.

XI. Facilities

This section provides information concerning the environment, or housing and materials needed to carry out the proposed project. It contains specific details and special features about the institution itself. Resources include special equipment, space, libraries, computer capabilities, services, and geographical locations.

Major equipment purchases and travel to or contact with other facilities should be spelled out and justified in this section. If cooperative agreements are being made to share facilities or personnel, the terms of agreement or contract authorization should be included.

XII. Personnel

This section identifies the principal people involved in the proposed project. Identify key personnel involved in the project, what their role(s) will be, and what percentage of time they will be working on the project. Clearly describe the project members' qualifications, skills, and areas of expertise. Include curriculum vitae (biographical sketches) of the major principal people in the Appendix section. (If names of key personnel are not yet known, include project responsibilities and methods of selection.) Give brief descriptions of other personnel, including key associates and consultants used in the project. State their educational qualifications, relevant experiences, professional memberships, honors, and recent and pertinent publications. If new personnel will be used for the project, include a job description.

XIII. Budget

The budget identifies all costs involved with the project and offers any explanation or justification for those costs. Clearly delineate the costs to be met by the funding source and those to be provided by the applicant and/or other parties. The budget is often a fiscal skeleton of the entire proposal and all items of the budget should be reflected in the proposal narrative. The budget figures should be justified, detailing how the numbers were derived. Current fringe benefits (20–30 percent) and indirect cost rates (8–15 percent) should be applied. Following are guidelines for direct and indirect costs associated with most projects.

Direct costs associated with project activities are usually broken down into the following categories:

1. Personnel: wages, salaries, and fringe benefit costs of professional and clerical persons employed full- or part-time in the project. Also, if the fiscal period extends beyond one year, merit raises and inflation adjustments (approximately 7 percent) apply.

2. Outside Services: consultant and service contracts. Consultant costs are usually short-term and include both travel and fees.

3. Supplies: consumable supplies used on the project for instruction and training.

4. Equipment: purchase and rental costs, as well as amounts allocated to maintenance and repairs.

5. Travel and Transportation: all travel and related subsistence costs directly incurred.

6. Communications: telephone installation and service; toll calls; messenger, cable, and telegraph service; and postage.

7. Publications: printing, publishing, and/or duplication of brochures, reports, reprints, and dissemination costs.

8. Other Costs: miscellaneous items not included elsewhere, such as computer time and necessary supporting services, facility rentals, and some fees.

Indirect costs are costs incurred in the general support and management of the activities; this is often called project overhead. Examples of indirect costs might include the following: general administration and general expenses such as accounting payroll and administrative offices; research administration; departmental administration expenses; and plant operation and maintenance, such as utilities, janitorial services, and repairs. (Often an 8–10 percent figure is used for indirect costs.)

Budget justification is necessary to explain and justify each nonobvious budget item requested. If there is any question about a line item, the explanation should clearly outline the purpose of and rationale for such items.

XIV. Appendixes

The appendixes should contain supporting information that helps to reinforce the basic arguments set forth in the project narrative sections. Supplemental data, graphs, charts, organizational and advisory council memberships, and curriculum vitae (resumes or biographical sketches) are examples of important data to be included. Letters from consultants or collaborators indicating their degree of involvement would also be provided here. Also, it is important to include the 501(c)(3) Non-Profit Statement of the Agency and previous year's annual budget. Appendixes should be numbered, in alphabetical order, and consistent with the table of contents.

Postapplication Process

Most proposals have a waiting period of notification which usually lasts from 2 to 6 weeks. Notification information and other important reporting procedures often are presented in a foundation's annual report or in the request for proposal (RFP) guidelines.

The proposal review process is conducted by knowledgeable and capable internal and/or external reviewers. The reviewers determine or evaluate a proposal according to specific guidelines and criteria which often are available from the funding organization.

Outcomes of the Proposal Review

Once the proposal has been submitted and is under review, a request for additional information can be made by either the reviewer or the grant seeker. Sometimes the funding source requests the applicant to modify the proposal, usually in terms of limiting project activities or decreasing the amount of funds requested. Modifications or compromises require serious attention, and revisions should be made without risking the integrity of the proposed project.

Occasionally a request is made by the funding source for a site visit to clarify details regarding staff, administration, facilities, or program peculiarities. Oral presentations can be an effective way to communicate ideas and suggestions for all parties involved.

If notification is given for the proposal's rejection, the agency may request details why the proposal was rejected. The criteria for evaluating the proposal is usually explained in the RFP.

SUMMARY

Seeking and obtaining grant monies is a vital part of any nonprofit organization. Yet putting together the proposal package with a viable idea is only part of the equation for success. To make the most of a proposal the organization must essentially get inside the head of the funding organization to address the need or perceived needs of the funder. This may be as simple as good public relations or as complex as a cooperative venture.

Activity 3.1 is a case study on grant proposal writing. The case follows the format used by federal agencies and includes the kind of organization and language typically found in federal RFPs. The EDCILL (Economic Development Through Community Initiative at the Local Level) Grant Writing Simulation provides a substantive understanding of how to develop a grant proposal including funding, interagency cooperation, and organization of services. Completion of this activity will allow participants to simulate the actual grant proposal process and will provide valuable insight into how they might work together as a team to develop real grant proposals.

ACTIVITY 3.1
EDCILL (ECONOMIC DEVELOPMENT
THROUGH COMMUNITY INITIATIVE AT THE LOCAL
LEVEL) GRANT WRITING SIMULATION

I. Planning

Goals: Upon completing this activity, participants will be able to identify the components of an RFP (request for proposal) and write and/or present a grant proposal in response to it.

Materials: Copies of the EDCILL RFP, Roles for the EDCILL Simulation Game, the demographics information, Appendix A, and Appendix B for each participant.

Time: Minimum of 3 hours.

Size of Group: 6 to 20 participants divided into groups of 3 to 5 people each.

Notes: This activity can be made as elaborate as desired. To reduce time and make the activity less involved, the facilitator may want to have the participants respond to only part of the RFP, develop only a brief outline of their proposal, and/or present the proposal verbally instead of in writing. To make the activity more elaborate and time intensive, the participants may be asked to develop a complete implementation plan for their proposal, a budget, and a written proposal.

II. Involvement

Step 1: A thorough review of Chapter 3 will help prepare the participants for this activity. This activity is most effective when the participants are knowledgeable about the grant writing process.

Step 2: The facilitator should decide which set of demographics (urban or rural) are to be used in the activity. Divide the participants into teams of 3 to 5 people each. Each team is to prepare a proposal in response to the EDCILL RFP. The teams may select agencies and organizations they wish to include in their proposal from the Roles for the EDCILL Simulation Game handout. To be more creative, teams may be encouraged to create their own agencies and organizations in addition to those listed in Roles for the EDCILL Simulation Game. Each team should be prepared to present their proposal (either in writing or verbally) at a designated time. To simulate a real RFP, fill in appropriate times, dates, and locations in sections 1.5, 1.9, and 1.10 of the RFP prior to distributing it to the participants.

Step 3: As facilitator, you should act as representative for the U.S. Department of Adult and Community Education and field questions from the participants to clarify the RFP and your expectations. It should be pointed out to participants that they do not need to conduct a needs assessment—that has been done and is presented in the form of the demographics (rural or urban). Be careful not to influence the design of the proposals with your responses.

Step 4: Allow sufficient time for each team to carefully develop its proposal. (For a shorter activity, have the participants make verbal presentations at a designated time, giving them about 1 to 1½ hours to prepare their proposals—see section 1.10 of the RFP. For a longer activity, have the participants prepare a written proposal to be presented at a later date.)

Step 5: Allow time for each team to present its proposal to the whole group (10 to 30 minutes per group for verbal presentations). Discuss the strengths and weaknesses of each proposal.

III. Reflection, Generalization, and Application

The participants should be encouraged to critique all the proposals from the standpoint of which are most likely to be funded. It may be useful to have a person who is knowledge-able about grant writing (or who has judged proposals) help to critique the proposals. Points to be made include how to read the various sections of the RFP, how to use the point scheme in Part II of the RFP, how to construct a budget, and how to plan the proposal using the time management chart in Appendix A of the RFP.

IV. Follow-up

The learning from this activity can be applied to real grant writing on the job. Participants may become members of a grant proposal team and be responsible for writing sections of a proposal under the direction of a more experienced grant proposal writer.

V. Activity

This activity may be reproduced for the participants.

EDCILL (ECONOMIC DEVELOPMENT THROUGH COMMUNITY INITIATIVE AT THE LOCAL LEVEL) REQUEST FOR PROPOSALS

PART I: GENERAL INFORMATION FOR CONTRACTORS

1.1   BACKGROUND. The Adult and Community Education Development Act (ACEDA) was signed into law October 1, 1998. The law provides funding to support economic growth through adult and community education activities. The act is administered by the U.S. Department of Adult and Community Education.

1.2 NOTE TO APPLICANTS. This notice is a complete application package to enable a contractor to submit a proposal for the ACEDA legislation which provides funding to support economic growth through adult and community education activities. The emphasis of this grant will be adult and community educational activities designed to support economic growth for economically distressed areas experiencing severe unemployment. Together, with the statute authorizing the program and applicable regulations governing the program, including the general administrative regulations of the U.S. Department of Adult and Community Education, this notice contains information, application forms, and instructions needed to apply for the *Economic Development Through Community Initiative at the Local Level* (EDCILL) program under this competition. To be considered, all responses to this Request for Proposal (RFP) must be submitted with an original and three (3) copies to:

Project Review Officer
U.S. Department of Adult and Community Education
Suite 224, Stouffer Hall
Washington, DC 01234

1.3 PURPOSE OF PROGRAM. This RFP provides contractors with sufficient information to enable them to prepare and submit proposals for consideration by the U.S. Department of Adult and Community Education. The purpose of the RFP is to promote local initiative toward developing economic recovery and growth in economically depressed areas. This goal is to be accomplished through activities such as the following: employment retraining, labor/community cooperation, community service, career development, literacy/basic skills, economic growth recovery of community, and revitalization of business and industry.

1.4   ELIGIBLE APPLICANTS. Nonprofit organizations and institutions such as institutions of higher education, hospitals, community agencies, school, and religious institutions are eligible to apply for funds through ACEDA. All applicants must be able to demonstrate a broad base of community involvement and support.

1.5   DATES FOR PROPOSAL APPLICATIONS
Deadline for Applications: _____
Deadline for Proposal Review: _____
Available Funds: $1,000,000 ($500,000 per year for two years).
Estimated Size of Awards: $1,000,000
Estimated Number of Awards: 1
Award Date: Programs are due to begin _____
Programs are due to end _____

1.6   APPLICATION REGULATIONS. The following regulations apply: The Education Department General Administrative Regulations (EDGAR) in 34 CFR, Part 74 (Administration of Grants to Institutions of Higher Education [IHE], Hospitals and Nonprofit Organizations), Part 75 (Direct Grant Programs), Part 77 (Definitions that Apply to Department Regulations), Part 79 (Intergovernmental Review of Department of Labor and Industry Programs and Activities), and Part 85. All contractors must comply with all Affirmative Action Assurances.

1.7   PROBLEM STATEMENT. The United States Government, under the leadership of the Department of Adult and Community Education, will make two year nonrenewable grants to eligible organizations and institutions. The proposal will be based upon a community economic feasibility study. The programs will be offered at public community agency facilities. To be eligible for the grant, an applicant must demonstrate that it has previously engaged in community service activities and that it has conducted other significant program(s) involving community outreach.

Applicants may apply for funds to hire support personnel to carry out the purpose of the proposal but may not use funds to hire additional continuing staff. Monies must be used to create new programs or to supplement existing programs for the purpose of this RFP. Monies cannot be used to continue existing programs.

1.8   ECONOMY OF PREPARATION. Proposals should be prepared simply and economically, providing a straightforward and concise description of the contractor's ability to meet the requirements of the RFP. Proposals, excluding the Budget section, should not be more than 10 typed pages, double-spaced, on one side of the paper, with 1-inch margins on all sides, using 12 point font size.

1.9   PREPROPOSAL CONFERENCE. A preproposal conference will be held on: _____. The purpose of this conference is to clarify any points in the RFP which may not have been clearly understood. Questions may be forwarded to the Project Review Officer, U.S. Department of Adult and Community Education prior to the meeting to ensure that sufficient analysis can be made before an answer is supplied. The preproposal conference is for information only. Answers furnished during this session will not ensure acceptance of proposals.

1.10   ORAL PRESENTATION. Contractors who submit proposals may be required to make an oral presentation of their proposal to the Project Review Officer of the U.S. Department of Adult and Community Education. Such presentations may eliminate the necessity for a typed document to be submitted and also provide an opportunity for potential contractors to clarify and defend their proposals. The Project Review Officer has scheduled these presentations for: _____. Each

contractor will have _____ minutes to present a proposal.

PART II: INFORMATION REQUIRED
FROM CONTRACTORS

Contractors' proposals must be submitted in the format outlined
below. To be considered, the proposal must respond to all requirements in this part of the RFP. Any other information
thought to be relevant, but not applicable to the enumerated
categories, should be provided as an appendix to the proposal.

2.1   ASSESSMENT OF NEED (10 points). State in succinct
        terms your understanding of the problem presented or
        the service required by this RFP. The needs should be
        limited to the problem(s) the contractor can resolve
        within the contract period. The problems should be sup-
        ported by appropriate documentation, including key sta-
        tistical information. Statistical information should be
        relevant only to the geographic area to be served.
2.2   MANAGEMENT SUMMARY (10 points). Describe the
        process by which the project will be managed to include
        the agencies/persons responsible for the administration
        of the project and how interagency cooperation to
        achieve project goals will be achieved. Also include a
        timeline, using a PERT chart, GANTT chart, or other
        appropriate format to display the required information.
        A suggested Management Timeline is included as Ap-
        pendix A.
2.3   QUALITY OF KEY PERSONNEL (10 points). Include
        the number of executives and professional personnel
        (analysts, auditors, researchers, programmers, consult-
        ants, etc.) who will be engaged in the work. Show where
        these personnel will be physically located during the
        time they are engaged in work. Include education and

experience in developing educational programs and conducting research. Indicate the responsibility each will have in this project.

2.4   PLAN OF OPERATION (30 points). Describe in narrative form your technical plan for accomplishing the work. The plan should include needs assessment; publicity and recruitment; goals, objectives, and activities for specific components of the project. Use the task description in PART III: WORK STATEMENT of this RFP as your point of focus. Modifications of the task descriptions are permitted; however, reasons for changes should be fully explained.

2.5   PRIOR EXPERIENCES (10 points). Include experience in the development of employment and educational programs, materials, and research. Studies or projects referred to should be identified, including the name, address, and telephone number of responsible officials.

2.6   PROGRAM EVALUATION (20 points). Provide evidence of program evaluation procedures which will demonstrate the value of the proposal to program participants, the objectives of the legislation, and the community.

2.7   PROJECT BUDGET SUMMARY (20 points). The information provided in this section is required to support the financial reasonableness of the proposal. Use Appendix B (Budget Worksheet) of this RFP to determine the budget request. This area will be weighed heavily; however, it will not necessarily be the deciding factor in the selection process. Among the allowable uses for funds are:

1. Personnel
   a. Salaries
   b. Fringe benefits

2. Operating costs
   a. Travel

    b. Consumable supplies

    c. Instructional and resource materials

    d. Administrative expenses

    e. Recruitment (brochure printing, publicity, advertising)

    f. Participant support costs

3. Physical plant and facilities

    a. Facility expenditures

    b. Utility and maintenance expenses (for each facility used)

4. Indirect costs (Administrative overhead associated with operating the program)

Nonallowable costs are as follows:

1. Computer hardware and software (unless specified as a major requirement of the proposal)

2. Capital improvement for existing physical plant facilities

3. Costs for space owned by the contractor

4. Personnel costs for persons not directly involved in the operation of the project

Ten percent (10%) of the total budget must be met through local level resources. This contribution can be met through capital, facilities, equipment, and in-kind contributions.

PART III: WORK STATEMENT

3.1   TASK DESCRIPTIONS. The following tasks are defined as being important to successful operation of any project funded under the EDCILL RFP. The task descriptions are as follows:

3.1A NEEDS ASSESSMENT. Describe in full the process of needs assessment used to establish (1) the general need of the community to receive funding under the ACEDA Legislation and (2) the specific needs on which the various components of the grant proposal are based.

3.1B PUBLICITY AND RECRUITMENT. Describe in full detail the methods used to publicize the program(s) and recruit the participation of (1) community agencies, (2) businesses, (3) educational institutions, (4) labor unions, (5) other institutions, and (6) participants for the project.

3.1C GOALS, OBJECTIVES, AND ACTIVITIES. Describe in detail the goals, objectives, and activities of each component of the project. The following are examples of possible components: vocational training, basic education and literacy training, economic transition assistance, business revitalization, research activities, job search assistance, and relocation assistance.

3.2 INTERINSTITUTIONAL COOPERATION AND COMMUNITY INVOLVEMENT. It is considered essential to the spirit of the ACEDA Legislation that cooperation among community agencies, educational institutions, businesses, labor unions, and other important local institutions be established. The spirit of community involvement on a broad scale is essential. The legislation calls for a broad-based community approach to the resolution of economic problems in severely economically depressed areas.

Appendix A: Management Timeline

Activity	July	Aug	Sep	Oct	Nov	Dec	Jan	Feb	Mar	Apr	May	Jun

Appendix B: Budget Worksheet			
Items	Amount Requested	Amount Contributed	Total
A. Personnel			
1. Full-time personnel			
a. Salaries			
b. Fringe benefits (@30%)			
2. Part-time personnel			
a. Salaries			
b. Fringe benefits (@15%)			
B. Operating costs			
1. Travel			
2. Consumable supplies			
3. Instructional materials			
4. Administrative expenses			
5. Recruitment (publicity & advertising)			
6. Participants support costs			
7. Equipment costs			
8. Other allowable costs			
C. Physical plant & facilities			
1. Facilities costs			
2. Utilities and maintenance			
3. Other allowable costs			
D. Other allowable expenses (include indirect costs)			
E. Total budget			

ROLES FOR THE EDCILL SIMULATION

Adams University School of Continuing Education. The mission of the School of Continuing Education at Adams University is to serve the lifelong educational needs of nontraditional students, working adults, professional organizations, local and state agencies, and the citizens of the community by providing access to the academic and human resources at the university.

Adams University Institute for Community Service. The mission of the Institute for Community Service at Adams University is to expand economic development in the community, serve as a base for the public service function of the university, and develop linkages between the university and the community. This is accomplished by identifying resources within the university and the community, bringing these together, and providing leadership and technical assistance in obtaining grants.

Adult Education Program. By looking to all the basic adult educational needs, the Adult Education Program provides quality education to adults 17 years of age or older in Jefferson County. The unit provides assistance in the areas of adult basic education, preparation for the GED, vocational and career counseling, academic assessment, and job readiness and search skills. There is sustained cooperative effort to support adult basic education in the county by working in cooperation with other organizations and agencies.

Community Action Agency. The mission of the Community Action Agency is to make the entire community more responsive to the needs and interests of the disadvantaged and to encourage self-sufficiency. This agency receives funding from a variety of sources, but does not receive government money. The agency's effectiveness is determined not only by the services directly provided but also by the improvements and changes encouraged in the community's attitudes and practices toward the disadvantaged.

Public Assistance Office. The mission of the Public Assistance Office is to promote, improve, and sustain the quality of family life, break down the cycle of dependency, protect and serve Jefferson County's most vulnerable citizens, and promote efficient management of the community's resources.

Job Center. Unemployment is a crucial problem in the community. The Job Center is designed to help the unemployed and members of their immediate families through a variety of services including peer and professional counseling, single point of contact, information, and referral. Programs include job placements, referral for classroom training, and job search skills training. The Center provides guidance, advocacy, and support to ensure maximum preparation for a new career.

Jefferson County Chamber of Commerce. The Chamber of Commerce works daily on the promotion of the business community and civic welfare of the county. The Chamber is committed to providing assistance in the following areas: developing existing business and industry; securing new industry suitable to the area; creating new jobs and new income; building pride and confidence in the community; maintaining information concerning the county; providing statistical services; and unifying local business and industry.

Payne Vocational/Technical School. Payne Vocational/ Technical (Vo-tech) School provides a variety of quality vocational courses and educational programs designed to meet the needs of the area's labor forces and business and industry. The school serves area high school students during the day and adults through evening and weekend programs.

Madison Manufacturing Company. This is a large local company that is concerned about the financial conditions in Jefferson County. It is concerned about the effect current economic conditions will have on future economic growth in the community.

Federation of Labor Unions. The Federation of Labor Unions is strong, active, and a vital part of the county's labor force. It represents a broad-based coalition of local labor unions. The president of the coalition (elected for a three-year term) has authority to speak for members of all the participating unions.

Franklin Community College. Franklin Community College has experienced rapid growth, especially with its non-credit, career-oriented programs for adults. The college is looking to position itself as a supplier of employees to local business and industry. The leadership of the community college is aggressive and the commitment to expansion considerable.

DEMOGRAPHICS FOR A RURAL SETTING

Jefferson County is one of 67 counties and is located in the southwest region of the state. From east to west, the county is about 23 miles wide. From north to south, it is about 37 miles long. The Census Bureau's population estimate for the county was 95,348 individuals. It is divided into 24 townships and 14 boroughs (towns). The county seat, Hamilton, has a population of 13,000 with the surrounding township's population of 15,000. Most of the available medical, social service, and job opportunities are located within a 5-mile radius of Hamilton. Yet, only one-third of the county's population lives within Hamilton and the surrounding township. Adams University is situated in Hamilton and has a student population of 15,000.

The county's most important natural resource and largest employer is the bituminous coal industry led by Washington Coal Company, the largest coal mining company in Jefferson County. This industry employs 8,000 individuals. However, it is experiencing economic difficulties and 1,200 employees have been laid off during the past year.

Pockets of natural gas are located all over Jefferson County. The various companies associated with this resource, collectively one of the area's largest employers, employ a total of 1,200 to 1,400 individuals dependent upon seasonal work. The gas industry is also experiencing economic difficulties and approximately 800 employees were laid off in the past year.

The other major employer in the area is Adams University, employing about 1,400 individuals in all levels from maintenance to instructional faculty. This is one stable source of employment not experiencing layoffs.

The county is rural and once enjoyed a large farming economy that produced hay, oats, and corn. Two products that are still effectively produced are potatoes and cabbage. Evergreen trees raised for export as Christmas trees are an additional profitable natural product.

According to state labor market estimates, more than 17,500 people in Jefferson County lived below the 125 percent federal poverty guideline. The 125 percent poverty guidelines are a household of two living at or below $835.00 per month/$10,020 per year and a household of four living at or below $1260.00 per month/$15,120 per year. This means that nearly 18 percent of the county's residents live in poverty. In recent years, unemployment has been a major problem in the county and in the surrounding counties. The county's jobless rate has gone from one of the lowest in the state 10 years ago to the second highest (10.7 percent) in the state in recent years.

Some of the major problems experienced in the county were identified through the local Community Action Agency's latest needs assessment survey of 1200 households (10,800 individuals). Those problems include: 20 percent indicated a lack of housing; 57 percent indicated a lack of employment; 36 percent indicated a lack of transportation; 64 percent indicated high utility bills; and 67 percent indicated the high cost of food.

DEMOGRAPHICS FOR AN URBAN SETTING

Jefferson County is one of 67 counties and is located in the southwest region of the state. The county's land area is 727 square miles (about 29 miles wide by 25 miles long). The Census Bureau's population estimate for the country is 1,450,195 individuals. The county is divided into 32 townships and 25 towns. The county seat, Hamilton, has a population of 383,000 (26 percent of the county's population). There are 80 communities surrounding Hamilton—each an independent town or village. Most of the available social service and job opportunities are located in the county seat or its surrounding districts. Nearly one-third of Jefferson County's population lives within Hamilton's 85 square mile area. Adams University is located in Hamilton and has a student population of about 30,000. Within the county, there are also two other universities, four colleges, one community college (consisting of three branch campuses), and three technical schools.

Not long ago, Jefferson County was a major manufacturing center. At one time steel, oil, and gas industries were the major employers. Due to the collapse of the steel industry, nearly 90,000 jobs were lost in the county within the last 15 years, and the population dropped more than 30 percent. The county successfully diversified its economy to avoid total economic collapse. Corporate centers, high technology, financial business, and other service industries have replaced steel, oil, and gas as the county's major employers. Even though major economic collapse was avoided, there are still areas within the county that could not avoid the wrath of the dying steel industry.

According to state labor market estimates, more than 218,000 people in Jefferson County live at or below the 125 percent federal poverty guideline (a household of two living at or below $835.00 per month/$10,020 per year and a household of four living at or below $1260.00 per month/$15,120 per year). This means that about 15 percent of the county's residents live in poverty. There are still many blue-collar residents and a large minority population in the county that could not successfully make the transition to the new highly technological economy. In fact, most of the high tech industries had to hire from outside the county.

Jefferson County has a higher percentage of people over 65 years of age than any other county in the nation. In spite of the county's economic problems, it has been consistently rated by the *Places Rated Almanac* as one of the best places to live. Hamilton also has a strong cultural environment.

One of the nation's largest current airport development projects is taking place in the county. Once the new midfield terminal is completed, at an expense of close to $600 million, Jefferson County will become a major hub in the nation's aviation system. This should also provide a major boost to the local economy.

CHAPTER 4

Enhancing Leadership Skills

What qualities do organizations demand of leaders? What qualities would people most like to exhibit if they held a leadership position? Kouzes and Posner (1987) polled managers, who identified the following traits (in order from most desirable to least): honesty, competence, forward-looking, inspiring, intelligent, fair-minded, broad-minded, straightforward, imaginative, dependable, supportive, courageous, caring, cooperative, mature, ambitious, determined, self-controlled, loyal, and independent. It could be very daunting to try and be everything a good leader should and it is easy to see why good leaders are in such short supply.

Masnerie (1996) also developed a list of the qualities of leaders based on a thorough review of the literature. She identified the following traits of effective leaders: they value coworkers; they seek improvements in the organization; they are risk takers; they develop and share a vision; they enlist the aid of others; they foster collaboration; they make others stronger; they set an example; and they recognize accomplishments.

As a result of their studies, Kouzes and Posner (1987) developed a list of five characteristics most often exhibited by leaders. The list included challenging the process, inspiring a shared vision, enabling others to act, modeling the way, and encouraging the heart. These actions all relate to the ability of the leader to create a climate where all members of the organization work together for a common goal.

The lists outlined above illustrate the emphasis on the personal qualities of effective leaders as opposed to the product or service knowledge of the organization. The latter kinds of knowledge, referred to as "technical knowledge," appear to be much less important than vision and people-related knowledge and skills.

For most adult and community education organizations this raises several questions: Can leaders effectively guide others through the budgeting roller coasters, inspire them to do their best, and meet the mission of the organization? Dean (1998) identified the six key tasks of leaders most relevant to adult and community education:

1. Developing a vision for the organization
   —creating the vision
   —inspiring staff to support the vision
   —providing an example to staff for following the vision
   —reinventing the vision as needed

2. Developing and enhancing ties to the organization's environment including
   —board of directors
   —funders
   —regulators
   —policy makers
   —competitors and collaborators
   —the public and the community
   —other politically significant individuals and organizations

3. Developing and enhancing professional development
   —assessing professional development, competence, and potential
   —providing professional development opportunities
   —creating a climate where professional development occurs on the job as well as in the classroom

4. Modeling effective interpersonal relationship skills with
   —staff

—clients/learners
—the public

5. Acquiring and managing information, including (but not limited to)
   —new sources of information
   —the field of expertise
   —trends in public policy and funding
   —leadership issues

6. Managing programs, projects, and budgets

Given the diverse nature of the activities outlined above, a broad range of skills and knowledge is required for a person to be an effective leader in adult and community education. Each of these will be explored in the following pages using the research and literature to help identify the underlying skills needed to be successful. First, however, the bases for the most often consulted leadership theories will be examined.

THE EVOLUTION OF CURRENT THEORIES OF LEADERSHIP

In this section four approaches to understanding leadership which have evolved over the last 70 years are explored. The first is the trait approach to leadership in which a universal set of effective leadership characteristics is emphasized. The second is the behavioral approach, where leadership is understood as consisting of a general style or consisting of certain behaviors. The third approach is situational leadership in which a combination of leader characteristics, subordinate characteristics, and the nature of the task are combined to help define the nature of the relationship between leaders and followers. The last approach to leadership is transformational leadership, which is understood to be a synergistic connection between leaders and followers where both are transformed. Learning more about each of these approaches to leadership adds to our understanding of leadership and enhances our ability to identify and capitalize on our own leadership strengths.

Trait Approach to Leadership

Leadership theorists began the century by turning to the social sciences. Initially, researchers believed that leadership was an inherited ability; they often described this position as "the natural born leader." The leader was one who was selected by God or the fates and led a charmed life. One could even say he/she was unlike other ordinary mortals. With this kind of thinking, it was futile to challenge the leader since he/she had "supernatural" sanctions and was, thus, destined for greatness (Borman, 1969, p. 244). Also, the concept of "charisma," possessing certain magic powers to inspire others, is a remnant of the early trait school of leadership.

The second premise of the trait approach to leadership was that if leadership traits could be identified, then these traits could be taught. Human behavior, however, cannot always be predicted or understood accurately. Some common identified leadership traits included originality, popularity, sociability, aggressiveness, desire to excel, humor, cooperativeness, liveliness, physical size, and athletic ability.

The trait theory of leadership lost favor as the realization occurred that people born into leadership positions were not always good leaders. According to Stodgill (1964), "A person does not become a leader by possession of some combination of traits, but the pattern of personal characteristics of the leader must bear some relevant relationship to the characteristics, activities, and goals of the followers" (p. 15). On one end of the scale, scholars studied certain traits which focused on the leader's tasks (organizational) with little or no concern for people. On the other end, some scholars were only concerned with people (relational). Peters and Waterman (1982) commented: "Although the trait approach may be useful in describing the leadership qualities required for a particular job, there are no universal agreements for effective application for all situations" (p. 13).

Leadership Styles and Behaviors

Viewing leadership as a set of behaviors arose as a reaction to the trait explanation of leadership. These sets of behaviors were grouped into several styles: authoritarian/directed, democratic/participative, or laissez-faire (free reign). Researchers eventually concluded that the task(s) to be accomplished, and group composition and environment/setting played important roles in the leadership style or the manner in which an individual performs actions that help a group to achieve mutually accepted goals.

The autocratic or authoritarian approach is used when time is a factor or when the group is inexperienced, unsophisticated, or unskilled, and when a quick decision by the leader is necessary. This style is seen as a pragmatic form of leadership which often emphasizes task accomplishment rather than group cohesiveness.

A second approach to leadership is democratic or participatory. People's needs are placed first and tasks are considered of secondary importance. The leader serves as a moderator or discussion leader eliciting ideas and suggestions from group members as they work together to determine actions to be taken. Group effectiveness, rather than efficiency, is considered the hallmark of the democratic style of leadership.

An example of the third leadership style, laissez-faire, is when the leader serves as the group facilitator or resource person. The group may appear ambiguous or "leaderless" until a leader is discovered or emerges from the process as the group works toward a designated goal. The laissez-faire approach is quite effective when the group is experienced, highly skilled, and self-motivated. However, laissez-faire leadership style is more time-consuming because greater management efforts must be taken individually by the group members. Pigors (1935) and French (1964) support these findings and they emphasize the importance of the organization and social system in the development of leadership. Both Pigors and French believe that leadership is not an attribute of personality (type) but a quality of one's role within an organization. Leadership is deter-

mined by the attitudes, general tone, and efficiency of the organization.

French (1964) further suggests that an effective leader
does not generally engage in behaviors that could be seen as self-
serving or egotistical. He believed that successful personnel policies and practices include effective staffing, a fair and equitable
compensation program, open avenues of communication and
appeal, training and development, appropriate attention to
physical and emotional health measures, and an environment
where fair play and integrity are emphasized. French lists several
behaviors that serve as guidelines for establishing effective leadership:

1. Leaders convey that they have confidence in their associates.

2. Leaders permit associates to have latitude in seeking solutions to work problems, whereby standardization in methods
   is not imperative.

3. Leaders encourage participation in managerial matters and
   goal setting.

4. Leaders practice effective planning and encourage associates
   to do the same. They also work at removing obstacles to
   achieving the group's goals.

5. Leaders use their associates' mistakes as learning and growth
   opportunities rather than opportunities for punitive measures.

6. Leaders are interested in their associates as total persons
   rather than as employees; their good work is recognized.
   Leaders do not play favorites but communicate information
   needed by their associates (pp. 536–538).

Situational Leadership

The situational theory or phase of leadership evolved primarily as a reaction to the failure of the trait approach and a
dissatisfaction with the behaviorist school perspective. The con-

temporary approach is to perceive leadership styles on a situational continuum resulting in the use of the "best" leadership style which is based on the following questions: What is the task to be accomplished? What is the group composition or skill level? What is the preferred role of the leader? The objective is to develop an awareness of the individual limits and the organizational resources, and the demands which the leadership process must address.

The Blake and Mouton (1964) studies with their managerial grid of leadership styles are good examples of situational leadership. The two-dimensional grid shows concern for people on one axis and concern for production on the other axis. This identifies the style of a leader, but it does not directly relate to his/her effectiveness. Reddin (1970), added a third dimension, "effectiveness" to the model. Reddin builds on the situational impact in that he believes that concern for people and concern for production can be effective or ineffective behaviors depending on the current situation. According to Luthans (1977), "Blake and Mouton's and Reddin's approaches to leadership seem prescriptive in some respect—but try to consider the situation, especially Reddin" (p. 448).

Hersey and Blanchard (1988) conclude that having only one single normative leadership style does not take into consideration such variables as cultural or societal differences, levels of education, quantity and quality of experience, or other situational variables. Further, none of the leadership authors spell out "how" a leader should act or what decisions should be made in a given situation.

Vroom and Yetton (1973) developed a normative model, "How to act as a leader in a given situation," which contains five leadership styles, seven situation dimensions, and seven decision rules. The leadership styles consists of variations of autocratic, consultative, and group styles. The situational dimensions consist of two general types: (1) the way in which problems affect the quality and acceptance of a decision and (2) the way in which the problems affect the degree of participation. A decision tree is used to determine various leadership styles from different situations. By answering each question carefully, the decision tree leads the person to the proper decision using the appropriate style of leadership.

Situational leadership theory then involves three major sets of variables: (1) the characteristics of the leader, (2) the role or characteristics of the followers, and (3) the dynamics of the situation or task to be accomplished. Situational leadership methods have been compared to the game of golf. Making the right shot (or decision) requires analyzing strengths and weaknesses of the person holding the club, or power, as is the case with a leader. The leader must be knowledgeable of the various techniques or styles available and choose the appropriate club for each specific shot. Further, the leader must be aware of the possible consequences when selecting a particular technique for application. Should the leader take risks and aim for the pin, or is playing it safe a better approach? The leader needs to know the situation and the technique before swinging away.

The key points in situation management are that different skills or techniques are required at each level because leaders are different, groups are diverse (some are highly skilled, others less sophisticated), and often the situations are unique, depending on such factors as time, deadlines, costs, resources, the job to be accomplished, the group, and the strengths and weaknesses of the leader. These variables all need to be considered in situational leadership.

Hersey and Blanchard (1988) developed the Leadership Effectiveness Attitude Description (LEAD) Questionnaire and the Situational Theory of Leadership from a synthesis of their earlier work at Ohio State Univesity. All of these factors are combined into the Life Cycle Model. The construct comprises four dimensions:

1. High task and low relationship—In this style the leader is *telling* employees what to do and how to do it. This style is most effective with new, unskilled, or inexperienced employees or when the task is new or unclear. High task in this sense refers to the leader focusing on the task so that employees can acquire the knowledge and skills to become competent on the job. Low relationship means that employees are gen-

erally not yet ready to offer advice or insight about what to do or how to do it, therefore the communication is usually one-way—the leader telling employees how to do the job.

2. High task and high relationship—As employees gain in competence, the leader's role shifts from telling to *selling* or *coaching*. In this role the leader still focuses on the task, making sure employees know what to do and how to do it, but also there is an emphasis on valuing the employees' input in making decisions and determining strategies to complete the task. The communication is two-way at this stage.

3. High relationship and low task—As employees continue to develop their skills as well as their confidence, the leader's role shifts again to *participating strategies* which emphasize the partnership relationship among employees and the leader. At this stage it is not necessary for the leader to continue preparing employees to master the tasks of the job, but it is important for the leader to nurture employees' growth and continued commitment to the job.

4. Low task and low relationship—As employees' competence and commitment continue to increase the leader is able to shift to a *delegating* role. At this stage the leader does not need to continually supervise employees' competence (high task) or monitor their commitment to the job (high relationship).

Activity 4.1, Taking the Lead, provides opportunity for exploring leadership styles and understanding how they influence the group process.

Transformational Leadership

The fourth and more recent school of thought, transformational leadership, suggests that trait leadership is not a transactional activity (that is, the leader searches for ways to persuade others to follow) but, rather, is transformational (others are inspired to follow because of a transformed perspective on life).

Transformational leadership theory suggests simply that people follow leaders because the leaders inspire them. Activity 4.2, Follow the Leader, emphasizes how leaders may operate when faced with the challenges of unplanned situations where relationships with followers are crucial for determining and reaching objectives.

Many descriptions of transformational leadership point to it as a strong focus. As Roberts (1985) explains:

> This type of leadership offers a vision of what could be and gives a sense of purpose and meaning to those who would share that vision. It builds commitment, enthusiasm, and excitement. It creates a hope in the future and a belief that the work is knowable, understandable, and manageable. The collective action that transforming leadership generates, empowers those who participate in the process. There is hope, there is optimism, there is energy. In essence, transforming leadership facilitates the redefinition of a people's mission and vision, a renewal of their commitment, and the restructuring of their systems for goal accomplishment. (p. 1024)

Transformational leadership consists of four important elements of practice: (1) idealized influence, (2) inspirational motivation, (3) intellectual stimulation, and (4) individualized consideration. Idealized influence refers to a leader appealing to follower's needs by using charisma and modeling appropriate behavior. Inspirational motivation refers to a leader who models the appropriate behavior, motivates, and inspires others. Intellectual stimulation has the leader questioning assumptions, reframing problems, and addressing old situations in new ways. Individualized consideration shows a leader paying special attention to each person's specific needs (Bass & Avolio, 1994). Transformational leaders move beyond a transactional relationship between the leader and follower to create a sense of common purpose among the team members (Bass, 1990; Burns, 1978).

Through their actions, transformational leaders stimulate team members to take deliberate action in a world of complex, ambiguous, and uncertain situations (Pfeiffer, 1981; Vaill, 1996). Therefore, leaders who have responsibilities for influencing or creating change must transform themselves from the traditional roles of managers to those of facilitators, coaches, and teachers where the creation and application of knowledge is fostered (Senge, 1990). If leaders wish to transform their organizations into institutions where organizational learning, knowledge creation, and application become integral parts of the culture, then leaders must reshape the culture in such ways so that the organization becomes a true learning organization (Nonaka & Takeuchi, 1995; Senge, 1990; Schein, 1985).

DEVELOPING LEADERSHIP SKILLS IN ADULT AND COMMUNITY EDUCATION

The discussion so far in this chapter centers on the research and theory of leadership. How does this apply to the role of leaders in adult and community education? At the beginning of the chapter six key roles for leaders in adult and community education were outlined (Dean, 1998). Each of these roles will be explored in more detail in light of current theory and research.

Developing a Vision

One of the exemplary leadership practices identified by Kouzes and Posner (1987) is inspiring a shared vision. The importance of this aspect of effective leadership has also been stressed by Cohen (1990) who stated that employees "are attracted to a leader's vision and future goals because they recognize that through them, they and the organization can become permanently better" (p. 33). Kotter (1990, 1991) reiterated this position by stating that the primary function of leaders is to produce change. Effective leaders are able to create a vision of the organization and the future and inspire others to work toward that goal. This element is critical to the success of the organization.

A vision is the culmination of experience in the field; knowledge of the organization, the environment, public policy, and the community; and a host of other factors all coming together in an intricate fashion to create a sense of the possibilities. The leader's vision must include both a goal that has not yet been attained as well as elements of the reality in which the organization exists. Too much "goal" and not enough "reality" will create an unrealistic expectation which staff will not buy into. Too much "reality" and not enough "goal" will send the message that we are not going anywhere and leave the door open to cynicism rather than optimism. Finding a balance that is right for the organization and the times is, perhaps, the leader's most important and most challenging task.

Having a vision is not the same thing as getting people to adopt it themselves. Also, adopting is not the same as "selling" the vision to employees. The staff do not want to be customers; they want to be partners with the leader. The important element of "inspiring a shared vision" is that the organization members adopt it because it is positive, indicates growth, is realistic, and includes them.

Enhancing Ties to the Organization's Environment

Enhancing ties to the organization's environment really consists of two activities: first is understanding the organization's relationships with other organizations and how to maintain and enhance them, and second is the more personal business of playing politics.

Understanding the organization's environment from the standpoint of its relationships with other organizations is covered in Chapter 2 in the sections on Assessing the External Environment and Categorizing Community Education Organizations. It is especially important that leaders be aware of changes in the organization's environment in terms of changes in government legislation and regulations, economic and demographic changes and trends, developments in their professions, local collaborators and competitors, and capitalizing on sources and opportunities. Keeping apprised of these quickly changing arenas can often be a full-time job.

Developing effective working relationships with boards and advisory councils is one of the more important functions of a leader in adult and community education as in most nonprofit organizations. In general there are two types of bodies to which the leader must relate. Although in actual practice these bodies go by many different kinds of names, they are distinguished here as boards and councils. A board is a body that has governing authority over the organization while a council functions more in an advisory capacity.

Some of the functions of boards include hiring the chief administrative officer and perhaps other key personnel, approving budgets, approving strategic or other administrative plans, and approving changes to the operations of the organization. There is great variety in the way board members are selected. Some are elected, some are appointed, some apply and are approved by other board members. In some cases board members must "buy" their seat through a donation to the agency. Councils, on the other hand, are usually more informal and membership is generally invited by the organization's leadership. Councils are used in a variety of capacities, usually to help the organization keep touch with other key organizations or people in the community it serves as well as help the organization generate new ideas.

According to Van Ness (1998a) the role and makeup of boards are changing. He outlines a number of key ways in which boards have evolved over the years. First, board members, in general, represent a more diverse socioeconomic and cultural background than they traditionally have. Second, boards tend to have more open relationships with the organization's staff. Third, board members are more likely to be chosen for their skills, not their social status. Fourth, boards are becoming less reactive and more proactive in creating vision and long-range plans for the organizations they serve. Fifth, boards tend to be less legalistic and more informal in their mode of operation and decision making. Sixth, there is currently a greater emphasis on achieving the mission rather than a control of funds as the primary function of the board. Seventh, there is an increase in board-staff interrelationships, especially in the area of planning. Eighth, there is less tendency to view conflict as negative. Instead it is seen as an opportunity to understand issues from different perspectives. Ninth, policies put forth by boards tend to be less restrictive and more enabling and flexible. Tenth, board business is viewed less as "weight" and more as exciting and challenging. Eleventh, board members used to be held accountable through unwritten or understood expectations; now more frequently there are written position descriptions and manuals for boards.

Van Ness's optimistic view of the changing nature of boards ties into his suggestions for creating more harmonious board-staff relations. His ideas (Van Ness, 1998b) are summarized here:

1. It is important for both staff and board members to remember they have a common goal and that they should work together to help each other rather than working independently or at cross purposes.

2. Both board and staff should continually remind themselves of their basic mission by asking this question: "How can we (each of these groups working together) achieve desired outcomes using available resources and valuing all personnel who carry out activities and programs to achieve those outcomes?"

3. Both boards and staff must be as clear as possible regarding their goals, roles, and relationships.

4. It is critical for staff to realize that the board has a legal responsibility to the stakeholders (usually defined as the taxpayers and the clients or the organization) to "establish legal and ethical policies that provide an enabling format for the accomplishment of the mission." Boards should realize that staff have responsibility to "carry out the programs and activities necessary to achieve the mission and respect the policies" of the organization.

5. Written agreements between boards and staff are just the starting point. In order to establish truly caring relation-

ships, both must exhibit "continual concern for the intangibles of respect, trust, integrity, and appreciation."

6. The most harmonious relationships (which are also the most effective as well as the most satisfying) are achieved when each group continually seeks to be supportive and helpful to the other group without interfering or meddling in the responsibilities of that group.

7. When disagreements occur (as seems inevitable when two groups with different roles work toward the same ends), "principled negotiating" (rather than positioned negotiating or, worse, unnegotiated backbiting) needs to be the standard operating procedure.

Establishing and maintaining a harmonious and productive working relationship with a board can be one of the more difficult tasks of a leader in adult and community education. This basic function is, however, essential for smooth operation and growth of the organization.

Enhancing Professional Development

Enhancing professional development of organization staff is one of the most critical functions because the nonprofit organization is only as good as its staff. Indeed, this is a basic premise of this book. Enhancing professional development can be divided into several interrelated processes: assessing staff to determine current levels of proficiency, locating appropriate professional development opportunities, encouraging participation in those opportunities, and creating a climate in the workplace for the transfer of learning from the classroom to the job.

Assessing the professional development of staff can be very anxiety producing especially when it is done with a traditional "performance appraisal" approach. Alternative approaches that include staff in the assessment design and implementation are less threatening, but more time consuming. A positive way to initiate evaluation is to have staff produce a report in which they cite their accomplishments and areas they feel they need to develop. The reviewer can then help the staff member think of ways to capitalize on these successes and continue with successful practices as well as enhance areas that are not as well developed. This approach takes the onus off administrators to find "problems" and takes most of the anxiety out of the process. It will still take a skillful administrator, however, to conduct a review with a person whose self-image is considerably different from that of the administrator.

As Galbraith and Zelenak (1989) have pointed out, there are several ways of engaging in professional development. They identified various forms of training: on-the-job training, in-service training, and graduate degree programs in adult education. In addition, attending workshops and conferences, reading the professional literature, and engaging in reflective practice could be added as strategies to enhance professional development. This book was designed as a supplement to in-service training opportunities. It provides a set of readings and activities on issues affecting adult and community education organizations today that can be used by members of an organization to initiate exploration of their own issues and concerns.

One of the chief concerns regarding training and professional development is "transfer of learning" from the classroom to the job. The issue for staff is that there is often a disparity between what they learn and what they are able to do on the job. Constraints such as lack of time, money, and supervisor support to try new ideas can be major roadblocks to innovation and improvement on the job. Stage 6, Application, of the Process Model for Experiential Learning in Adult Education (Figure 1.1) emphasizes the transferring of new learning to the job. Stage 7, Follow-up, stresses the need for continued interaction among staff and administrators on the job to ensure that transfer of learning occurs. The most important aspect of this process is to provide a climate on the job in which staff feel comfortable in applying what they have learned. This must be a climate of trust in which staff are not unduly criticized for mistakes, a climate in which they can try new ideas on the job without fear of recrimination.

Modeling Interpersonal Relationship Skills

Followers respond more to what leaders do than what they say. If we think of the leaders we have known in the past, it becomes obvious that we remember most how they treated us, not their words or speeches. Referring again to the list of attributes of effective leaders compiled by Masnerie (1996) it will be noted that six of the nine attributes refer to enhancing leader-follower relationships. These attributes are valuing coworkers, enlisting the aid of others, fostering collaboration, making others stronger, setting an example, and recognizing accomplishments. Nanus (1989) notes that "the strongest, most durable and substantial parts of an organization are the satisfaction, commitment, and sense of direction shared by members of the organization. These intangibles are the real test pillars of the organization" (p. 50). According to Cohen (1990) the essence of leadership "is to motivate people to perform to their maximum potential to achieve goals or objectives" (p. 15). Drucker (1990), noted that effective leaders reflect those characteristics most employees view as important in order to gain their commitment and trust. The message appears to be that true leaders not only need a vision but also need to be respected as people by the followers before they will actually follow them.

More specific interpersonal relationship skills include coping with conflict in the organization and dealing with upset people, whether they be employees, clients, or the public. Conflict resolution is an area that has received a lot of attention in the literature. Miall (1992) points out that conflict prevention is different from conflict resolution. If the expectation in the organization is cooperation, then the need for conflict resolution diminishes because the opportunity for conflict itself is diminished. When conflict does occur there are many barriers to successful resolution. Arrow, Mnookin, Ross, Tversky, and Wilson (1985) identified three broad categories of barriers to conflict resolution: tactical and strategic barriers, psychological barriers, and institutional or organizational barriers. Tactical barriers arise from the efforts of bargainers in conflict situations to maximize their short-term and/or long-term outcomes. Often people will conceal their true intentions and/or priorities to accomplish this. Psychological barriers are characterized by the biases with which people interpret information, evaluate risks, and set priorities. Conflict resolution is an interactive social process in which people make inferences about the motives and character of each other. Examples of institutional barriers are bureaucratic structures that restrict the flow of information and politics that restrain people from making decisions or compromises that might resolve the conflict.

Many different approaches to conflict resolution have been proposed. Miall (1992) identifies the conditions under which conflict resolution is most likely to be successful in an organization: (1) open communication channels, (2) opportunity for parties to air their grievances and relieve anger and frustration, (3) the presence of a third party who has the trust of both sides, (4) the making of gestures on both sides to indicate serious intent to resolve the conflict, and (5) the use of existing procedures within the organization. Sandole and Van der Merwe (1993) stated that conflict can be resolved if both parties adopt the appropriate attitudes. These attitudes include (1) the willingness to put forth the effort necessary to work through the differences, (2) sufficient commitment to overcome obstacles that arise in the process, (3) the ability to explore alternative meanings for ideas and events, and (4) the willingness to participate in the mutually creative process that occurs during successful conflict resolution.

Dealing with clients, staff, or members of the public who are upset is another function that leaders are often called upon to do. Creating open communication in these cases must precede any serious attempt at more formal conflict resolution. Blanchard (1990) has proposed a five-step process for dealing with people who are upset, angry, or frustrated. First, he says we must listen to the other people and allow them to say their piece. To cut them off or try to impose our own view before they have released their feelings will only heighten any sense of anger or resentment they have. Second, we should empathize with how they feel. This does not mean we must agree with their understanding of the situation, but we need to at least recognize that they have a right to be upset and to express their feelings. Third, once the person or persons are calmed down enough to engage in a rational exploration of the situation, we can attempt to clarify the facts with them. As important as this stage is, it can only occur after the feelings and emotions have been addressed. Fourth, after the facts have been clarified, then we can engage in problem solving, brain storming, or other action to help identify alternatives to resolving the conflict situation. Last, we need to agree to take action with the other parties. This may involve the setting of goals and deadlines for accomplishing them.

Many different approaches to conflict resolution have been proposed. However, they all have one aspect in common: handling differences and working toward win-win solutions is the key to success. Activity 4.3, A Course of a Different Color, underscores the important roles leaders play in facilitating collaboration, communication, and conflict resolution in a group.

Acquiring and Managing Information

A key factor in the success of an organization is the quantity and quality of the information that goes into decision making in the organization. While the types of information and the sources for such information will vary with different organizations, there are several broad areas in which most adult and community educators need to be informed. These include government and legislative activities, economic and demographic changes, developments in the profession, local competitors and collaborators, and funding sources and opportunities.

There are as many sources of information as there are types of information to be acquired. Because any one source may result in information in several different areas, no attempt is made to list sources by the type of information they may yield.

Listservs

There are many different listservs and other computer-based sources of information available. Some of the more relevant listservs are identified here based on a compilation by Zengler (1998): AEDNET is an international network of individuals interested in adult education; NIFL-ALLD (National Institute for Literacy) is a listserv focusing on adult learning disabilities; NIFL-Family (National Institute for Literacy) is focused on family literacy; NIFL-Workplace (National Institute for Literacy) focuses on workplace literacy education; NLA (National Literacy Advocacy) provides information about legislative and public policy issues; and Numeracy is focused on numeracy education.

Internet

The World Wide Web has opened a vast arena for acquiring information. Zengler (1998) offers a few key Internet addresses for adult and community educators: **http://hub1.worlded.org/** is a site for the Adult Literacy Technology Hub, Region 1 (eastern states) and is focused on the needs of adult literacy educators; **http;//ericae2.edu.cua.edu/search.htm** provides access to the 16 ERIC Clearinghouses to do literature searches; **http://coe.ohio-state.edu/cete/ericacve/index.htm** is the site for the ERIC Clearinghouse on Adult, Career, and Vocational Education; **http://www.ed.gov/** offers information about the primary federal education agency; and **http://www.nald.ca/** is the Canadian site for literacy education.

Conferences, Workshops, and Professional Organizations

Because of the proliferation of conferences and workshops sponsored by professional associations, no attempt will be made to present a comprehensive list. Instead, some of the more important professional associations and their respective conferences will be mentioned to provide a sample of the many opportunities available. At the national level there are several organizations that should be mentioned. The American Association for Adult and Continuing Education (AAACE) is an umbrella association under which a number of commissions and units are housed. These include the Commission on Adult Basic

Education (COABE) which sponsors a journal, *The Journal of Adult Basic Education*, and a national conference each year. AAACE also sponsors a national conference each year, usually held in October or November as well as two publications, *The Adult Education Quarterly* and *Adult Learning*. The National Community Education Association (NCEA) also sponsors a yearly conference as well as two journals, *The Community Education Journal* and *The Community Education Research Digest*. There are several state and regional journals also of interest. The Pennsylvania Association for Adult Continuing Education (PAACE) publishes the *PAACE Journal of Lifelong Learning* and the Rocky Mountains-Plains Adult Education Association publishes the *Rocky Mountains-Plains Journal of Adult Education*.

In addition there are several conferences each year that are not directly sponsored by a professional association but draw support from a variety of sources. Two of these are the Midwest Research-to-Practice Conference in Adult, Continuing, and Community Education and the Adult Education Research Conference. Pennsylvania (and perhaps other states as well) has identified eight regions in the state, each of which sponsor a number of professional development activities throughout the year. These are focused on adult basic and literacy education and are excellent opportunities for getting informed and networking.

Managing Programs, Projects, and Budgets

Administrators in adult and community education are required to wear many hats to accomplish their jobs and keep their organizations on track. The activities they face in any one day may include meeting with politicians, helping a client, writing a grant proposal, and even changing lightbulbs. Seldom in a smaller agency is the distinction clearly drawn between leadership and management functions in the organization. Of the six general areas of leadership identified in this chapter, the first five are primarily leadership functions. The last one, managing programs, projects, and budgets, is primarily a management function. Since the management function of administration is covered extensively elsewhere (and is much too broad a topic to cover here), this discussion is limited to discerning the distinctions between management and leadership. For a more in-depth discussion of the management functions in adult and community education, the reader is referred to Chapter 5, Planning and Implementing Effective Programs, and Chapter 7, Managing Volunteers: From Recruiting to Retaining. In addition, readers are referred to *Administering Successful Programs for Adults: Promoting Excellence in Adult, Community, and Continuing Education* by Galbraith, Sisco, and Gugliemino (1997) for a thorough discussion of management functions in adult and community education.

The differences between leading and managing have been drawn by many authors. Perhaps the first to bring this point home was Drucker (1967) when he made the distinction between "doing the right things and doing things right" (p. 2). Later, Bennis (1989) used this phrase to distinguish between management and leadership when he said that leaders do the right things and managers do things right. The distinction is effectiveness in the former case and efficiency in the later case. A motto for an army unit once read: Take care of the small things and the big things will take care of themselves. This phrase epitomizes the essence of management: pay attention to details and make sure everything is operating the way it is supposed to, and the rest will fall into place.

It has been noted that even in major corporations most people in management need to be able to function as both leaders and managers (Bolt, 1989; Kelly, 1991; Kotter, 1990; and Lee, 1989). It has also been noted, however, that the same skills are not required for both functions. Kotter (1990) stated, "Some people have the capacity to become excellent managers but not strong leaders. Others have great leadership potential but, for a variety of reasons, have great difficulty becoming strong managers" (p. 4). Adult and community education administrators are generally called upon to function as both leaders and managers. Often promoted through the ranks to positions of leadership, adult and community education administrators may come to the job with strengths in some areas and weaknesses in others. Herein lies a great weakness in adult and community education: our leaders often have the experience and knowledge to function well as managers but lack the kind of training and exposure that molds great leaders. They are often forced to learn to be leaders on-the-job, using a trial and error approach that can be difficult for the even the most self-assured individual. Ongoing professional development is one way to meet this challenge.

SUMMARY

The contents of this chapter suggest that leaders are made not born. Successful leaders acquire the skills necessary to perform the required tasks to get the job done. In effect, leadership is a function of interacting with people, where one person's actions directly affect others.

Matching a leader's talents to the tasks, however, is not enough to ensure success. The success of a leader depends upon the cooperative support of the followers. This interaction increases loyalty and encourages further participation and involvement. In sum, a leader is a teacher, an influencer, and a catalyst for action and results.

The following activities will provide opportunities for exploring and understanding leadership styles and how leaders influence others. Activity 4.1, Taking the Lead: Informal Group Leadership Assessment, helps participants to identify and critique their leadership styles. Activity 4.2, Follow the Leader: Rotating Discussion Leaders, provides opportunities to lead a discussion in a small group. Activity 4.3, A Course of a Different Color: Group Dynamics Role Play, allows for personal and interpersonal development while practicing leadership behaviors such as collaboration, communication, and conflict resolution.

ACTIVITY 4.1
TAKING THE LEAD: INFORMAL
GROUP LEADERSHIP ASSESSMENT

I. Planning

Goals: Upon completing this activity, participants will be able to identify and critique their leadership styles.

Materials: Paper and pencils.

Time: Approximately 1 hour.

Size of Group: From 12 to 16 people divided into groups of 3 to 6 people each.

II. Involvement

Step 1: Divide the participants into small groups of 3 to 6 people each. Allow about 5 minutes without further instructions. Let them talk or do what they wish as long as they stay together as a group. The groups may discuss any topics they choose; there are no limitations on the choice of topics. Do not answer questions or provide assistance; let the groups find their own way.

Step 2: After 5 minutes ask each participant to join a new group. Allow time for interaction. Follow this procedure two more times (for a total of four small group interactions), but answer questions and provide assistance as needed.

Step 3: Give each participant paper and pencil. Instruct each person to divide the paper into two columns. Explain that in one column they should list the topics that were discussed during the small group periods. In the next column they should list the topics they would have liked to discuss. They should cross out each topic that appears in both columns.

Step 4: Once the lists have been completed, ask each participant to find a partner. Together they are to go over their lists and help each other identify ways they could have directed the group discussion to include their interests.

Step 5: Conduct a whole group discussion in which participants reflect on the small group discussions they just experienced and identify examples of how a leader in the workplace gains involvement and commitment of group members.

III. Reflection, Generalization, and Application

The debriefing should include a discussion about what each group did in the first session. What was discussed? How did they feel? Was there a process? These are all questions to initiate discussion. Contrast their feelings and experiences with the last session. What was different or similar? Participants may relate having had feelings of anxiety and uncertainty. Indicate that you intentionally ignored them in the early stages to represent lack of management support. Share that it is common to have these kinds of feelings in group situations, especially when there is not a designated leader. Elicit or make the learning point that anyone can become a leader in a given situation—and to be successful requires open communication.

IV. Follow-up

Participants should realize that there are varying leadership styles. They will see that how well they influenced others during the exercise is an indicator of their ability to lead without a formal role or position of authority. Emphasize that in the exercise and back on the job, there are different leadership styles required for various situations and that by being aware of their leadership qualities, participants will be prepared to lead the way to success.

V. Activity

The exercise is conducted verbally, so there are no additional materials needed.

ACTIVITY 4.2
FOLLOW THE LEADER:
ROTATING DISCUSSION LEADERS

I. Planning

Goal: Upon completing this activity, participants will be able to lead a discussion in a small group.
Materials: None.
Time: 45 minutes to 1 hour.
Size of Group: Approximately 10 to 20 people divided into groups of 4 or 5 people each.

II. Involvement

Step 1: Divide participants into small groups of 5 each. Assign a number (1 to 5) to each member of each small group. The participants are to remember their number, and when they hear their number called they are to lead a discussion on any topic they choose. Each discussion is to last approximately 2 minutes.

Step 2: Call the numbers in random order (for example, 3 may be first, followed by 1, 5, 4 and 2, or any other order). The participants will not be aware of the order until the numbers are called.

Step 3: After everyone has presented a topic, have participants discuss in small groups what is involved in being a discussion leader. Starter questions might include: How did I prepare before my number was called? How did I select a topic? How did I feel when I didn't get a response?

III. Reflection, Generalization, and Application

Participants will learn that communicating in groups and one to one is an important component of being an effective leader. Intangibles such as rapport, humor, wit, and poise are just a few of the traits that leaders possess. Emphasize that practice—in workshops, at home, and on the job—is the easiest way to improve their leadership skills.

IV. Follow-up

As a follow-up activity, participants may be asked to research a quality improvement topic for the organization and make a presentation to a committee or panel. This will allow them to practice leading discussion groups and, at the same time, generate money-saving ideas for the organization.

V. Activity

This activity is conducted verbally, so there are no additional materials needed.

ACTIVITY 4.3
A COURSE OF A DIFFERENT COLOR:
GROUP DYNAMICS ROLE PLAY

I. Planning

Goals: Upon completing this activity, participants will be able to understand group dynamics and the roles various members play, as well as group leadership behaviors such as collaboration, communication, and conflict resolution.

Materials: Markers, index cards, flip chart or chalkboard.

Time: 30 minutes.

Size of Group: 8 to 12 people (roles may be deleted).

II. Involvement

Step 1: Distribute one index card (with a role written on it) to each participant and tell them not to share the information on their index card with others in the group.

Step 2: Indicate that the purpose of the exercise is to select a color for the group, and that each person should role-play according to the information on the card. Tell the group to begin the selection process.

Step 3: After 15 minutes have elapsed, indicate that the group must choose a chairperson, someone who has remained neutral and unbiased.

Step 4: Allow 15 more minutes, then ask for their color choice.

III. Reflection, Generalization, and Application

Ask participants to reflect on how people play various roles in a group. Emphasize that individuals often speak from a position of a strong vested interest. Discuss how difficult it is for people to compromise, change positions, or communicate effectively when they let their individual interests drive the discussion. Effective leaders need to recognize that everyone has different opinions and ideas about issues that arise. Individuals who learn how to influence others, negotiate for their interests, and work with others to achieve solutions will recognize desired results. Indicate that participants should now be aware of different "styles" in group settings, as well as how to deal with conflicting or diverse ways of thinking when interacting with others.

IV. Follow-up

Ask participants to identify leaders and group participation styles in a variety of settings (for example, work, community, church) and to relate the lessons of this activity to understanding how leaders in those situations function.

V. Activity

Before conducting the exercise, become familiar with the roles participants will play in the exercise. Then, print each of the roles and responsibilities on a separate index card (as follows). Each role should be written on a different index card. Provide one card to each person.

ROLES FOR A COURSE OF A DIFFERENT COLOR

Role: Information Seeker (Ask many questions during the process.)—Position: Support blue.

Role: Tension Reliever (Make jokes or laugh when things get too serious.)—Position: Introduce a different color, orange.

Role: Clarifier (Attempt to help people understand other's points of view.)—Position: Support red.

Role: None *(You know that the group is going to be asked to select a chairperson later in the exercise. You remain neutral so that they will select you as chairperson.)*—Position: None.

Role: Gatekeeper (Ensure each person is given a fair chance to express an opinion.)—Position: Against red.

Role: Initiator (Be enthusiastic about the group making progress and keeping on track.)—Position: Support green.

Role: Observer/Judge (Remain quiet and take notes about what transpires during the process.)—Position: None.

Role: Follower (Agree with everyone, especially when a leader arises in the group.)—Position: Against red.

Role: Information-giver (Provide directions, time constraints, goals, etc.)—Position: Against blue.

Role: Harmonizer (Try to keep everyone at ease and happy.)—Position: Against green.

Role: Coordinator (Express the need to get on task and make a decision in the allotted time.)—Position: Support blue.

Role: Summarizer (Repeat or paraphrase what other people say.)—Position: Support red.

CHAPTER 5

Planning and Implementing Effective Programs

During the coming years, the forces of politics and negotiations, economics, technology, competition, and organizational culture will become increasingly recognized as major factors influencing the designs of educational programs. Adult and community education organizations will find it increasingly important to understand both the internal and external forces that affect planning. Adding value and quality to products and services is a key function of program planning. It could be argued that planning is another "P" to add to the traditional four "P's" of marketing—price, product, place, and promotion—advocated by marketing experts and economic developers.

"Planning [in management and organizations]," according to Koontz, O'Donnell, and Weihrich (1986) and updated by Weihrich and Koontz (1993), is "Selecting missions and objectives—and the strategies, policies, programs, and procedures for achieving them; decision making; and the selection of a course of action from among alternatives" (p. 717). Sork and Caffarella (1989) suggest that "Planning refers to the process of determining the ends to be pursued and the means employed to achieve them. In adult education, planning is a decision-making process and a set of related activities that produce educational program design specifications for one or more adult learners" (p. 233). As these closely allied definitions suggest, planning today—and in the future—is no longer an isolated series of activities but, rather, a complex set of procedures.

Cardoza (1996) added that this transformation from a series of activities to a complex set of procedures demands not only a new institutional paradigm, but more importantly, the participation of highly skilled professionals to assure high rates of technical change. He stated: "Innovate or perish is the statement that best defines the present situation" (p. 9). Planning is, then, an interactive process, a dialectic among organizers and constituents, much like power negotiations from the boardroom to the classroom or from the union hall to the assembly hall. As Cervero and Wilson (1994) suggest, program planning is a social, political, and participatory process. Planning should empower the stakeholders and participants to discover alternative realities through a give-and-take process of negotiated interests.

Most traditional program planning models for adult education and training are linear in design. A review of the literature (Houle, 1972; Knowles, 1980; Koontz, O'Donnell & Weihrich 1986; Pennington & Green, 1976; Sork & Buskey, 1986; Tyler, 1949; Weihrich & Koontz, 1993) reveals sequential steps in most program planning designs:

1. Assess needs.

2. Establish program priorities and responsibilities.

3. Select program goals and objectives to address suitable themes.

4. Allocate available resources.

5. Select appropriate implementation techniques (strategies).

6. Evaluate results or outcomes.

7. Determine the program's effectiveness (accountability).

THE PROGRAM PLANNING WHEEL

The Program Planning Wheel (Murk & Walls, 1996) addressed in this chapter is a newly developed planning construct, an evolution of the Systems Approach Model (SAM) (Murk & Galbraith, 1986). The wheel through its inherent design continues the original SAM concept as an integrated, nonlinear approach to program planning. The Program Planning Wheel, shown in Figure 5.1, gives planners a hands-on working tool to create and evaluate the components of a program. The wheel also explains the program planning process through a model that closely simulates actual practice, which often is like juggling. While all the balls in the air are of equal importance, the balls on the way down get most of the juggler's attention. So it is with program planning and evaluation. The Program Planning Wheel provides a model in which the planners, like the juggler keeping several balls in the air, can handle several tasks or assignments simultaneously.

Each of the primary components of the wheel has subdivisions which provide key interrelated, interdependent modules. In Figure 5.1 the spokes of the wheel are numbered for reference to the labels in the caption. In the real world of program planners, these activities do not always follow a sequence. In fact, the purpose of the wheel is to emphasize the interelatedness and nonsequentiality of these activities. The primary components of the program planning process highlighted in the wheel are:

- Internal and external influences
- Evaluation and follow-up
- Educational process determinants
- Needs assessment
- Instructional planning
- Administrative and budget development
- Program development and implementation

Planning an educational program for adult learners or with community developers is not as orderly or predictable as some would like it to be. It essentially involves politics, many compromises, and negotiating interests (Cervero & Wilson, 1994; Cookson, 1998). As a result, planning is not always logical or sequential. It is not possible to say that one will always conduct a needs assessment prior to developing curriculum or planning activities. In some cases, needs assessments may be politically inappropriate given the desires of funders or other decision makers. The following descriptions of each section of the Program Planning Wheel provide planners and developers with ideas and strategies to assist them as they consider the particular circumstances they face in their organizations and communities.

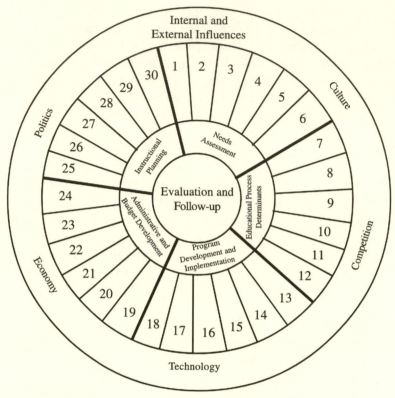

Figure 5.1 The Program Planning Wheel. With permission of Peter Murk.

Key to Spokes of the Wheel
1. Establishing existing priorities
2. Categorizing existing programs
3. Studying community structure
4. Developing survey instruments and questionnaires
5. Identifying participant preferences
6. Determining participant goals and experiences
7. Participating in a group activity; developing group skills and talents
8. Certifying a skill or talent
9. Practicing a skill; producing a product
10. Improving a skill; learning by doing
11. Learning what to do and acquiring new skills
12. Understanding; acquiring knowledge
13. Offering appropriate recognition and rewards
14. Monitoring the program and accommodating special needs
15. Activating the program
16. Creating and launching a promotional campaign
17. Organizing support staff
18. Producing instructional materials
19. Substantiating the priorities as determined
20. Coordinating existing resources and programs

21. Corroborating with the organizational mission and structure
22. Writing a grant proposal and acquiring external support
23. Determining an ample fee structure
24. Formulating a cost-effective budget
25. Coordinating facilities and staff
26. Scheduling people, time, and facilities
27. Recruiting effective instructors and resources
28. Selecting appropriate learning activities
29. Identifying program outcomes
30. Defining program purposes

Hub of the Wheel: Evaluation and Follow-up
• Addressing and dealing with internal and external influences
• Designing progressive evaluation instruments and techniques
• Reiterating and reviewing program mission and goals
• Identifying and correcting problem areas and concerns
• Evaluating instructional objectives
• Determining instructional effectiveness
• Obtaining constructive criticism

Internal and External Influences

Internal and external influences are depicted as constantly revolving around the outer part of the wheel and therefore constantly affecting the planning process. Program planning is never done in a vacuum. There are always political, economic, and cultural realities to consider. The major influences are competition, culture, economy, politics, and technology, all of which impact the planning process both internally and externally. It should be noted that the constituents or consumers of the educational program are not listed in this section even though they are, in many respects, the ultimate influencers. Because of their direct influence, they are addressed in the planning wheel in the Needs Assessment section.

Internally, the influences are typically interrelated. Competition occurs between individuals and/or departments, each competing for limited resources. One department or group may have more technology or might be better equipped to use the available technology than another, thus garnering greater support for its program.

Externally, the influences can be interrelated as well. Competition for funding might be the single most continuous force facing any organization. Politically, programs can gain or lose federal or state funding depending on which political party is in office or if the budget is cut for existing programs. Further, organizations may develop an edge when they use technology to its fullest extent. For example, using computer on-line services, the Internet, and interactive television as vehicles for developing and delivering new educational programs may make some programs more competitive than others.

Evaluation and Follow-up

The components of evaluation and follow-up are at the hub of the wheel to graphically illustrate that this is a central function to each of the spokes. Continuous evaluation and follow-up functions are the core to successful program planning. Planners cannot wait to perform these functions at the end of the planning process, as is implied in a linear or sequential model. The planning strategies listed as evaluation and follow-up and found in the hub of the wheel include the following:

- Addressing and dealing with internal and external influences
- Designing progressive evaluation instruments and techniques
- Reiterating and reviewing program mission and goals
- Identifying and correcting problem areas and concerns
- Evaluating instructional objectives
- Determining instructional effectiveness
- Obtaining constructive criticism

Addressing and dealing with the internal and external influences are key issues in evaluation and follow-up. Especially noteworthy are such evaluative strategies as reviewing the program's mission and goals—to ensure that the planners are on track and in sync with their organization's mission (what they are currently doing) and vision (where they want to go). Second, using the strategy of correcting problem areas (perhaps identified from previous programs assessments) and dealing with concerns (voiced by supervisors, managers, or senior participants) are influencers which might indicate the direction that the new program should follow. Finally, obtaining constructive criticism provides effective feedback to consider as new plans are made.

Educational Process Determinants

The educational process determinants help program planners to identify and determine individual characteristics that the program has been designed to serve. This section plays an important role in helping the planners conceptualize some of the influences, externally and internally, and to determine how they will be addressed. This section also enables the evaluation process to measure and follow up on individual outcomes instead of simply reviewing a program as a whole. The educational process determinants section is subdivided into the following components:

- Understanding; acquiring knowledge
- Learning what to do and acquiring new skills
- Improving a skill; learning by doing
- Practicing a skill; producing a product
- Certifying a skill or talent
- Participating in a group activity; developing group skills and talents

As planners utilize the strategies of the educational process determinants component, they should ask the following three questions: (1) What is the purpose of, and/or rationale for, the adult and community education program? (2) What instructional form and/or curriculum design for acquiring new skills, improving skills, or practicing skills will work best with this program? and (3) What direction or special curricular emphasis should be taken?

Needs Assessment

The needs assessment component focuses on the who and why elements and is subdivided as follows:

- Determining participant goals and experiences
- Identifying participant preferences
- Developing survey instruments and questionnaires
- Studying community structure
- Categorizing existing programs
- Establishing existing priorities

In determining a needs assessment, it is important for the planners to be cognizant of the major reasons why (expectations and perceived benefits) people should or would want to attend the program. A second issue centers on who (the targeted population) should attend. Determining the desires of the target population can be attempted through formal needs assessment techniques such as community-wide surveys, special questionnaires, sampling techniques, focus groups, and telephone marketing. Informal needs assessment procedures can also be used, which include having informal discussions, reviewing topical issues found in newspapers, magazines, or trade journals, and relying on personal networking.

As assessment data is compiled both formally and informally, planners should carefully inventory the strengths and resources of their community and organization. In doing so they should ask some key questions: What are the support structures? Who are or might become the "champions of the cause"? What kinds of programs would be most beneficial? What times and locations would be most convenient? Who might serve as qualified instructors, supervisors, and support staff for the program? What are the major resources available in terms of agencies, personnel, and financial support so as not to duplicate but to coordinate efforts? What separate programs that currently exist might be coordinated under the new program planning effort?

Instructional Planning

The instructional planning section focuses on program design. This section again addresses and conceptually deals with the influencers, internally and externally, by reviewing and reflecting on the overall purpose(s), outcomes, scheduling, and coordination of initiatives and functions. This section is subdivided into the following components:

- Defining program purposes
- Identifying program outcomes
- Selecting appropriate learning activities
- Recruiting effective instructors and resources
- Scheduling people, time, and facilities
- Coordinating facilities and staff

Dean (1994b) in *Designing Instruction for Adult Learners* identifies several questions for assessing the various contexts affecting the learning activity: What is the mission and purpose of the sponsoring organization(s)? What are the line, staff, and functional relationships in the sponsoring organization? How are decisions made, and who makes them? What are the norms, values, and attitudes of the people in the sponsoring organization? How does the learning activity (program) enhance or support the organization's mission and purpose? Does it match the values and norms of the organization? Are there sufficient resources (financial, personnel, etc.) available to support the learning activity?

Dean (1994b) also indicates that the goals for the program can be developed based on desired learning outcomes (from a task or content analysis), from learning contexts, from an instructor's strengths and needs, or from the learners' observed or expressed needs. Developing appropriate (programmatic) goals and objectives is an important planning strategy and will aid in developing effective learning activities.

Another instructional planning component is selecting effective instructors and resource persons with the appropriate qualifications and credentials. Often, it helps to have written testimonials of instructors' previous work and documentation of their academic success. Enthusiasm and special sensitivity to the needs and interests of adult learners are important requisites for selection. Ongoing faculty evaluation and staff development strategies are highly recommended to ensure quality instruction. Identifying and implementing the program logistics, which includes facilities coordination, audiovisual techniques, and the "correct" scheduling of time, sites, and staff, are also important activities in instructional design and planning (Murk & Galbraith, 1986).

Administrative and Budget Development

The administrative and budget development section focuses on the costs and financial support for the program and is generally subdivided into the following components:

• Formulating a cost-effective budget
• Determining an ample fee structure
• Writing a grant proposal and acquiring external support

- Corroborating with the organizational mission and structure
- Coordinating existing resources and programs
- Substantiating the priorities as determined

Kowalski (1988) views the budget as "a document outlining a plan of financial operations. Specifically, it sets forth an estimate of proposed expenditures for a given period or purpose and the proposed means of financing those expenditures" (p. 162). Budgets are generally classified as program budgets, which list the projected income and expenses of a particular endeavor, and line item budgets, which are listings of income and expenditures categories assigned to lines on a page. Knowing the fixed and variable costs associated with programs are important program considerations (Galbraith, Sisco & Guglielmino, 1997).

Planners should not rely on fees alone for supporting their programs but should seek additional funding resources such as (1) organizational subsidies, (2) grants and contracts from foundations, (3) funding from the federal and state sources, (4) other funding sources (often in-kind) and (5) auxiliary enterprises, for example, the sale of materials and publications (Caffarella, 1994). Planners address and deal with internal and external influences, corroborating with the organizational mission and structure, substantiating the priorities as determined, and coordinating existing resources to avoid duplication and to gain internal support, commitment, and the organization's dedication for the program's success. All planning activities should be coordinated under a strong financial plan of action and budget. According to Galbraith, Sisco, and Guglielmino (1997), "Because of the nature and mission of most organizations in adult and community education, program budgeting has become the preferred approach to sound financial management" (p. 64).

Program Development and Implementation

The program development and implementation section focuses on activating the program and developing accountability measures. This section is subdivided into the following components:

- Producing instructional materials
- Organizing support staff
- Creating and launching a promotional campaign
- Activating the program
- Monitoring the program and accommodating special needs
- Offering appropriate recognition and rewards

The business of getting a program up and running is largely a matter of exercising effective leadership skills, which is addressed in Chapter 4. A key element often forgotten in the implementation phase is promoting the program. A successful promotional campaign may need more developmental strategies than just advertising. All promotional variables need to be employed. In addition to advertising (any paid form), the following should be evaluated and considered: publicity (unpaid reports by journalists in newspapers, magazines, radio, or television, such as public service announcements); sales promotions (discounts for early registrations or for registering or attending with a friend); personal selling (face to face); and packaging (linking programs together, offering self-directed learning options, offering the program through a television network or distance learning initiative).

Internal and external influences are addressed through the overall promotional activities and monitoring during which planners address the specific needs of clients, make adjustments in the program, and practice accountability measures—all which help programs to be successful.

Implementing a successful program requires constant coordinating and monitoring efforts by the planners. As in any well-planned program, unexpected crises do occur—in scheduling, staffing, or accommodations—so the planners need to be aware, ever vigilant, and able to make the necessary adjustments. It is better to plan for surprises than to be surprised.

SUMMARY

This chapter has emphasized the use of the Program Planning Wheel in Figure 5.1 as a working model to help planners of educational programs for adults. The Program Planning Wheel is a hands-on tool for a systems approach to planning. This systems approach is adaptable to multiple settings, serving the various needs of administrators and developers, instructors and trainers, and corporate users, as well as the planners.

The flexibility, creativity, and practicality of the wheel also facilitates the planning process. The Program Planning Wheel encourages a creative approach to program planning, and provides both a macro and a micro systems approach to planning. The wheel addresses the internal and external influences such as dealing with politics and power, the economic variables, technology, organizational culture, and competition. Finally, it addresses the contextual realities of organizational expectations, and the constituent and societal needs as well.

Activities 5.1 and 5.2 will provide the readers with opportunities to apply the concepts of the Program Planning Wheel in different scenarios. Activity 5.1, Easturbia Case Study, presents the reader with the challenge of developing a program to meet the needs of a suburban community while Activity 5.2, Sandstone Community Case Study, focuses on the needs of a rural community. In both case studies, participants are asked to develop a comprehensive approach to addressing the educational needs of these communities.

ACTIVITY 5.1
EASTURBIA CASE STUDY

I. Planning

Goals: Upon completing this activity, participants will be able to apply the Program Planning Wheel to identify one or more solutions to the case study.

Materials: Pencils, paper, Program Planning Wheel, and copies of the case study for each participant.

Time: 1 to 2 hours.

Size of Group: Individuals or groups of up to 15 people.

II. Involvement

This case study is presented in two parts. First, the description of Easturbia appears. Second, discussion questions are presented to stimulate thinking about the case study. This case study can be approached in two ways. First, participants may assume the role of Mary Beth Carpenter, the main character. In this scenario all would work together to try to find solutions to the case study from her perspective. Second, participants may each assume different characters in the case study and stage a meeting or series of meetings to discuss the development of an adult and community education program in Easturbia.

III. Reflection, Generalization, and Application

The Easturbia Case Study describes a situation not unlike many suburban communities, which has several benefits. First, participants can gain insight into the dynamics of a typical suburban community. Second, participants can gain experience in applying the Program Planning Wheel to an actual situation. Discussion of the case study can focus on how the situation was analyzed, what was learned about the situation in Easturbia, and how well the Program Planning Wheel worked as a model for understanding the situation in Easturbia. Participants can transfer their understanding of the uses of the wheel to their own communities and program planning situations. The program Mary Beth Carpenter is being asked to develop in Easturbia is a comprehensive approach to adult and community education for a community. More often, program planners will be developing programs on a smaller scale, designed with a more limited impact in the community.

IV. Follow-up

Use the Program Planning Wheel to analyze current or future programs developed by your agency. What aspects of program planning come to light as you apply the wheel that may not have been clearly identified previously? How well does the wheel apply to your situation? Who could or should be involved in the planning?

V. Activity

The following case study may be reproduced from the book and distributed to participants.

EASTURBIA: A SUBURBAN COMMUNITY WITH A RAPIDLY CHANGING POPULATION

Easturbia is a suburban community with a population of 45,000. It is a bedroom suburb of Main City, a large metropolitan area with a population of 200,000. Fifty years ago, after the death of heiress Mabel Stanford, the land and properties of Raintree County were bequeathed to the community. Through the efforts of Fred J. Mathews, the president and CEO of Mathews & Associates, Developers, Easturbia had its beginning. Most of the homes are in the $150,000 to $210,000 range, but to the consternation of many, some apartments designed for families of "middle class means" who work in the fast food and service industries, are springing up in several parts of the community. For this reason, the zoning board is a center of political controversy. There is practically no industry in Easturbia. Few of the residents make their living there, most of them being executives, businesspeople, corporate types, and professionals, who commute daily to their offices in the adjacent metropolis of Main City.

Retail business establishments, however, are increasing as business firms continue to decentralize into certain sections of the town. The population of Easturbia is growing rapidly. Many of the residents moved out of Main City to escape perceived social and racial tensions that were arising as a result of the congested population in the urban metropolis. Morning and evening traffic congestion is rapidly reaching a crisis stage. The population of Easturbia is both socially and economically homogeneous.

Juvenile delinquency and vandalism, according to Chief John Black, has shown a sharp increase among middle class and upper class families, probably due to a lack of direction or things to do. Easturbia is a young community and has no organized program of adult and community education. The school superintendent, Dr. Will Parker, has administered a few avocation classes from time to time in answer to occasional requests. The public university in Main City offers some evening classes. Other urban social agencies, however, are doing very little to aid the residents of Easturbia.

Easturbia has a fairly good public school system as well as a strong parochial school led by the Rev. Theodore J.

Thompson, pastor of the First Lutheran Church. A building program occupies much of the time of Dr. Parker and Ruth Ann Wilson, who chairs the Easturbia Board of Education. Mary Richards, vice president of the First National Bank, has mentioned that taxes in Easturbia are high and civic loyalty to the community is not very strong. Something definitely needs to be done.

The Parent Teachers Association, led by Bobbie Sue Tucker, is quite active and very responsive to the community's goals. Recently, in answer to the popular demand for a more comprehensive education program for the adults and teens of Easturbia, the Easturbia Board of Education hired Mary Beth Carpenter as the full-time director of adult and community education.

Dr. Parker, however, is not totally convinced of the wisdom of spending the community's hard-earned tax money for adult education. The school superintendent believes that such money should be used to educate the younger children of the community. Nevertheless, he has agreed to give it his support, but only on an experimental basis.

One of the many tasks faced by the citizens of Easturbia is the need for careful community planning and development if they are to create and maintain the kind of community which they deem desirable. Connie Green has been a vocal force advocating the need for community planning.

Discussion Questions

Here are some questions Mary Beth Carpenter may need to address as she implements a new adult and community education program for the Easturbia community.

1. What are the unique problems a community of this type faces when attempting to develop a total adult and community education (cooperative) program?

2. Describe the three most important and/or pressing problems which this community faces. What might be alternatives or possible solutions? How should these problems be addressed?

3. Should the adult and community education program only be concerned with enrichment, recreation, and academics or should it try to address the other community problems?

4. How should Mary Beth Carpenter, or anyone else, proceed when developing a new and creative adult and community education program for the Easturbia community?

5. Should an advisory council be created? If so, who should be the members?

6. What role should Mary Beth Carpenter, as the school system's director of adult and community education, play in this planning process? What role should the newly created advisory council play? Why?

7. What other questions should be raised?

ACTIVITY 5.2
SANDSTONE COMMUNITY CASE STUDY

I. Planning

Goals: Upon completing this activity, participants will be able to develop a program development model and rationale for implementing adult and community education on a community-wide basis.

Materials: Pencils, paper, Program Planning Wheel, and copies of the case study for each participant.

Time: 45 minutes to 1 hour.

Size of Group: Up to 20 participants in small groups of 3 to 5 people each.

II. Involvement

Step 1: Ask participants to read the Sandstone Community Case Study.

Step 2: Place participants in groups of 3 to 5 persons each. Indicate that each group will now discuss the case study and respond to the tasks at the end.

Step 3: Once the small groups have had an opportunity to discuss the case study, reconvene the whole group and conduct a large group discussion.

III. Reflection, Generalization, and Application

Discussion with the entire group will relate the case to the real world. Participants' responses to the exercise should focus on the specific model, components, and rationale for their models based on their experiences. Emphasize that these processes and concepts are the same as those used back in the workplace.

IV. Follow-up

It may be productive to have participants identify opportunities in their own community for expanding existing resources or overcoming limitations. Using the skills practiced in this exercise, participants may learn to take a new look at old problems and possibly uncover more effective ways of doing work, obtaining resources, and enhancing the organization.

V. Activity

The following case study may be reproduced from the book and distributed to participants.

SANDSTONE COMMUNITY CASE STUDY

Sandstone is located in the largest mining belt in the world. A large majority of the town families gain their livelihood from the quarry industry, others from the shops of nearby cities. The families of the adjacent rural districts depend on their farms. There is a grocery store, a tavern, an auto repair shop, and an insurance agency in town. These enterprises and the public school complete the list of agencies that afford employment to the residents of this area.

Since most of Granite County lies in this sandstone quarry district, and all the sections are within commuting distance of industrial cities, this area is typical of other rural school districts in the county. The area consists of a small incorporated town of approximately 850 people and the rural districts immediately bordering it. The public school is centrally located and is a modern sandstone building with ample space for its present enrollment.

This community has the usual adult organizations typical of small towns. There is a town council and mayor, four churches and their various organizations, the American Legion and Ladies' Auxiliary, the Parent Teachers Association, several lodges, and several social clubs. There is no public library in the community and the high school library is inadequate; there is no cinema, and there is no YMCA or any other recreational organization.

The social problems of this area are not much different from those of other small communities. The leaders of the community hesitate to advance what they judge to be untested principles and would rather sit back and let well enough alone. The social structure of the town is very closely knit with neighbors quite intimate and somewhat dependent upon each other. No agency offers adult or community education worthy of the name, other than the county agricultural extension service which has a few individual contacts with the farmers. There is no organized farm group in the community.

Under a new state plan, you have been hired to create adult and community education opportunities for Sandstone. You report to a state commission, which has provided resources for a needs assessment. While you do not report directly to the school board or the mayor and city council, these are important bodies with whom you must work in order to be successful.

Tasks

1. Develop a general approach to assessing the resources and limitations of the community.

2. Identify the resources of the community.

3. Identify the limitations of the community.

4. Identify the desired outcomes of adult and community education programs in the community.

5. Develop a structure (or organization) to initiate adult and community education in the community.

CHAPTER 6

Resolving the Community Dilemma: Fostering Interagency Cooperation

The concept of agencies and organizations joining together to achieve more than any one agency could accomplish alone is always appealing in principle. By combining and coordinating forces, unified action takes place, and the group's potential for providing community services becomes greater than individual efforts. It makes sense to work together for the benefit not only of the constituents, but also for the agency personnel.

Unfortunately, bringing people together from various agencies can create many different problems and conflicts as they work toward a common purpose. Personality clashes, conflicting values, divergent goals, ineffective communication, threats to status or persons, unequal efforts and benefits—these are just some of the issues that may have to be addressed.

There is no question that it is often easier to work alone. However, the complexities of our society, combined with scarce personnel and diminishing financial resources, compel us to work together on many projects. According to Van Ness (1981), the benefits of people and agencies working cooperatively clearly outweigh the difficulties. Cooperation requires that each party relinquishes something (that is, a part of its autonomy) as it gains something, which is a willingness to share responsibilities and develop trust in other people. Cooperation is not as "neat and clean" or as simple as working alone, but it can be more effective and produce greater results.

Van Ness suggests combining efforts and developing a better understanding of interagency cooperation. When an agency works by itself, it will avoid risks or threats, protect its resources, get sole credit for its efforts, and control goals, methods, and efforts. However, when agencies cooperate, they can prevent duplication of effort and overlapping of services, economize and stretch resources, multiply the efforts of personnel and facilities, serve clientele more effectively, increase public support for all agencies involved, and achieve goals unreachable through individual efforts.

ILLUSTRATIONS OF INTERAGENCY COOPERATION

Today in business and industry, collaboration is the buzz-word for making vision become reality. Many businesses, social services, and community groups benefit from interagency cooperation and special partnerships.

According to Byrne, Brandt and Port (1993), businesses are forming temporary linkages, partnerships, and alliances to attain their goals. These entities, called the virtual corporation, are a temporary network of independent companies—suppliers, customers, even competitors—linked by information technology whose purpose is to share skills, costs, and access to one another's markets (p. 99). The authors cite numerous examples of strategic alliances, such as AT&T using Japan's Marubeni Trading Company to link up with Matsushita Electric Industrial Company to jump-start the production of its Safari notebook computer. Another example is IBM, Apple Computers, and Motorola using an interfirm alliance to develop an operating system and microprocessor for a new generation of computers.

Taking a page from its corporate cousin, the nonprofit sector has had its share of collaborative successes. For instance, in Floyd County, Indiana, an Alcohol and Drug Task Force coordinates community-wide efforts to address the problems of substance abuse. These endeavors, which require strong linkage with public and private organizations, involve hundreds of community volunteers in all stages of the planning.

In addition, agencies in Warsaw, Indiana, began a Latchkey Program to provide a safe, after-school environment for children from three elementary schools. Goals mushroomed through the

efforts of volunteers and the local United Way into an enrichment program which involves people providing bus transportation, field trips, speech and physical therapy, health screening,
and staff in-service.

Another illustration of cooperation is the Coalition of
Human Service Planning Council, a loosely bound group of
funding agencies in Indianapolis, which shares information
about their activities and ventures and has created an entity
called Community Services of Indianapolis, which receives federal funding and provides greater services to Indiana's citizens
in need (Katz, 1991). And the list continues to grow.

These are but a few examples of the myriad ways in which
volunteers are cooperating to achieve results. But is this just a
fad, or a legitimate way to help the thousands of interagency
and cooperative programs to exist and prosper?

UNDERLYING ASSUMPTIONS
FOR COMMUNITIES

Global markets and increasing technologies have driven
corporations around the world to revamp how they do business.
It is no different on the local community level, where dwindling
resources, increasing needs, and common goals necessitate taking a new approach. According to Shoop (1984), there are a
number of assumptions that underscore the need for cooperation among all the agencies in a given community:

1. Economically, it is often unsound to duplicate existing facilities in a community.

2. Cooperation is preferable to competition.

3. It is logical to serve one need well, rather than to serve many
   needs partially.

4. There is more need for services in any given community than
   there are services available.

5. Needs change within a community.

6. Needs within a given community differ from person to person.

7. There are many services that have logical relatedness and mutual benefits.

8. People for whom the services are designed should be provided with opportunities to participate in making decisions affecting the delivery systems of services.

DEVELOPING INTERAGENCY COOPERATION

Necessity often creates unique and sometimes strange partnerships in the business world. Before an organization commits to a collaborative approach, however, it should consider all of the benefits and drawbacks to doing so. How the collaboration begins may well indicate the degree of success for everyone concerned.

According to Murk (1994), several important methods for developing cooperation exist. He claims that to get off on the right foot and stay on track, it is necessary to do the following:

• Show the greater needs of other agency's people, not just the designated agency's need, through an annual needs assessment (for example, an agency review).
• Demonstrate how cooperation can enhance or expand existing efforts and eliminate duplication of efforts or programs.
• Make the cooperative efforts simple and inexpensive, such as through regular contacts in meetings and frequent communications via telephone, mail, and electronic mail.
• Develop a client-centered focus, with informed leadership that helps develop a shared vision, a plan that delineates shared goals and objectives, and appropriate agency representation on the team to execute the plan (Imel & Sandoval 1990).

Brunner (1991) suggests other cooperative strategies as well, such as jointly developing and agreeing to common goals and directives, sharing responsibilities for obtaining those goals, and working together to achieve those goals, using the expertise of each collaborator.

Organizations that develop positive relationships with each other leave the door open for future cooperation when the time is right or circumstances demand linkages such as developing joint funding measures for programs. Interagency cooperation is both possible and practical when organizations are willing to work with *all* groups and agencies and not at the exclusion of reluctant or unwilling organizations. Activity 6.2, Join the Club: Community Exercise, stresses the importance of open communication and collaboration when a diverse group works toward a common goal.

Barriers to Cooperation

Although it appears on the surface that cooperating on common initiatives makes sense, many negative forces can both inhibit and deter interagency cooperation. Some come in the form of personal bias, others from traditional ways of doing things. The "Terrible T's"—time, trust, turf, and tradition— often top the list of deterrents to cooperation. Here are some other common inhibitors that prevent agency and organization cooperation:

- Competition for resources, recognition, or status
- Lack of ownership or input regarding the mission or central purpose
- Organization structure and/or insecure leadership
- Unequal power bases; differing value systems, priorities, or concerns
- Past negative experiences with cooperating
- Perceived threat to persons or to the agency
- Hidden agendas, misinformation, and red tape
- Fear of failure, personal resentment, jealousy, and damaged egos

- Legal jargon or constraints, racism, sexism, or ageism
- A win-lose attitude or resistance to change
- Lack of a sense of true community

That so many barriers exist would seem to indicate that seeking to collaborate with other organizations is a lost cause. Yet, there are many ways to overcome barriers while creating a successful joint venture. Activity 6.1, Community Dilemma, is a potent illustration of how failure to identify with the whole community can lead to factions and turf wars while expansive thinking can help create a viable sense of the whole community.

Keys to Gaining Cooperation

By adopting a "can do" attitude, an organization can avoid many of the pitfalls to developing a collaborative relationship with other agencies or groups. Many positive characteristics can promote interagency cooperation measures. An organization can begin to engender a sense of trust and commitment to the greater cause long before the project starts. For instance, it helps to do the following:

- Develop common goals, seeking mutual benefits and concerns for clients. Promote more efficient and effective use of facilities, personnel, materials, and finances.
- Get to know persons individually within another agency. Use good communication skills and build bridges of trust.
- Convince the organizational leadership through demonstrated examples that it is mutually beneficial to cooperate.
- Develop and demonstrate mutual trust and mutual concerns. Foster supportive relationships and assure others that no one will be undercut by the merger of time, talents, and agencies.
- Create a sense of ownership by all parties. Demonstrate a willingness to compromise. Develop a positive attitude for working together on common projects.
- Know and understand the purposes, goals, and missions of the other agencies and organizations. Work to identify com-

mon goals and objectives to serve the clientele. Look toward
the future when developing long-range goals.

- Be flexible. Seek common understanding and be willing to ac-
  cept additional training and staff development, better agency
  cooperation, and leadership development.
- When possible, develop an advisory council or board of directors from all agencies involved to share mutual concerns, discuss common problems, and work toward finding solutions
  and avenues for future cooperative measures.
- Work toward joint/collective funding projects which will be
  mutually beneficial to all agencies involved.
- Share resource files, assessment techniques, monitoring procedures, and evaluation techniques.
- Above all, develop a true sense of cooperation and community.

A Plan for Better Cooperation

Knowing what barriers exist and how to get around them
is a step in the right direction when seeking cooperation from
other agencies or groups. Janove (1984) suggests developing a
Plan of Action for more effective interagency cooperation. The
following actions will help ensure a smooth start-up and ongoing efforts for all parties. As a rule, each agency's staff must do
the following:

1. Make a thorough assessment of its mission, responsibilities,
   and activities, asking, What aren't we doing that we should?
   What are we doing that we shouldn't? What are the most important activities that we should conduct to fulfill our mission? Each agency must then prioritize those activities.

2. Identify those activities for which the agency believes it is
   totally responsible. Laws, community expectations, and policies place demands on agencies and their boards of directors
   that define areas of uniqueness. Agencies that are aware of
   their unique responsibilities save themselves and others much
   wasted and inappropriate effort.

3. Strive to identify and meet with the staff of other agencies, organizations, and institutions that appear to share similar goals, responsibilities, interests, and activities.

4. Collaborate to identify similar areas of concern and develop plans to cooperate, implement, and evaluate the programs and activities.

5. Attempt to increase the number of agencies and specific activities involved.

6. Continue to assess its own purpose, mission, and goals, and evaluate and assess cooperative efforts.

CYCLIC PROCESS MODEL
FOR DEVELOPING STRATEGIES

A viable technique for developing strategies and seeing them through to fruition is the process model developed by Janove (1984). This six-step model, which is cyclic in nature, begins with a general assessment and continues on to final evaluation of results. See Figure 6.1.

Phase One of the model requires *Assessment.* The purpose of assessment is to determine where your organization is or what conditions exist that warrant change. Assessments (both formal and informal) identify the group's purposes, determine information that is needed, clarify the process of gathering data in relationship to goals and available resources and set priorities.

Phase Two involves *Setting Realistic Goals* to meet determined needs. A goal is defined as a positive statement that describes what need is to be met or which community conditions are going to be changed. Alternative solutions are identified and those thought to be achievable are listed as objectives.

Phase Three, *Formulation of an Action Plan* includes:

• Strategies to reach specific objectives and to attain goals
• Identification of people, groups, and agencies that should be involved, and strategies developed to enlist their cooperation
• Examination and exploration of existing community re-

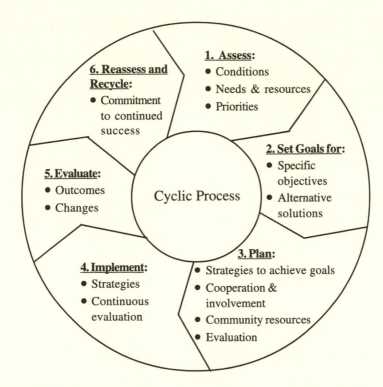

Figure 6.1 The Cyclic Process (adapted from Janove, 1984). With permission of Ethan B. Janove.

sources—human, financial, and physical—to determine how they are currently influencing and impacting on the problem, and to project how they could possibly be involved in solutions to the problem

- Evaluation procedures that examine the action plan to ensure that it is comprehensive, coordinated, and attacking the whole problem, not just part of it
- Evaluation strategies for the next phases

Phase Four is the *Implementation of the Action Plan.* The strategies are now put into motion with special attention given to ensure that people know what they are to do and by when. Assignments of responsibilities with deadlines for accomplishing tasks are clearly delineated and determined. In addition, the evaluation strategies developed during Phase Three are implemented.

Phase Five is *Evaluation.* Activities are identified to determine whether strategies are taking place as planned and whether they are having the desired effect. If the answers are negative, immediate changes are made to attain the desired goals.

Phase Six involves *Reassessment and Recycling.* These processes take place when strategies, activities, and/or programs are completed. This phase entails a review of the present situation. Then the cyclic process continues.

SUMMARY

The Mott Foundation (1975) developed a community education training film entitled *2 + 2 = 6—Interagency Cooperation,* which describes synergy and mutual collaboration through interagency cooperation. The combined results of people with goodwill and integrity can far exceed the efforts of most dedicated people working diligently but alone.

With scarce human, financial, and agency resources, the need for interagency cooperation has never been greater. The idea that agencies working together can do a better job of serving the needs of people than they can by working alone is the most important assumption underlying the concept of interagency cooperation. Agencies are more efficient, greater numbers of individuals are helped, and, consequently, communities are better served when people and agencies cooperate.

The two simulation exercises which follow, Activity 6.1, Community Dilemma, and Activity 6.2, Join the Club: Community Exercise, can be effective ways to begin developing interagency cooperation in your community. Community Dilemma is a powerful activity in which the participants have the opportunity to learn the true meaning of *community.* Join the Club emphasizes meeting management and interpersonal relationship skills, the necessary building blocks to initiating interagency collaboration. These activities demonstrate how decisions are made and how cooperation is often obtained. Further, the activities point out the importance of group dynamics, hidden agendas, and how people interact in high stress situations. These activities are but the beginning on a long road to greater agency effectiveness where the whole is greater than the sum of the parts.

ACTIVITY 6.1
COMMUNITY DILEMMA

I. Planning

Goal: Upon completing this activity, participants will be able to understand the nature of intercommunity and intracommunity conflicts and the value of using a win-win approach in conflict situations.

Materials: Flip chart or chalkboard, 5×8 index cards, markers, and score sheets.

Time: Approximately 1 hour to 90 minutes.

Size of Group: 12 to 24 people divided into groups of 3 or 4 people each.

II. Involvement

Step 1: Explain that the object of Community Dilemma is to score the maximum number of positive points. Refer participants to the large group and small group score sheets.

Step 2: Distribute a small group score sheet to each participant and two 5×8 index cards to each small group. Each index card is labeled A or B. The group number is also written on the card as indicated in the diagram below.

A	B
Group 1	Group 1

Step 3: Tell each group that scores will be posted on the large group scoring sheet where they will be visible to all participants. The large group scoring sheet may be drawn on poster paper or a chalkboard or displayed on an overhead pro-

jector. Indicate that groups will have 3 minutes between rounds to decide which card (A or B) they wish to play.

Step 4: Instruct participants to begin discussing which card they will play. After 3 minutes, collect the cards from each small group. Place the cards in an envelope so that other groups cannot see which card has been played. Announce the cards played by each group and record the appropriate scores on the large group score sheet. Repeat this process for Rounds 2 and 3.

Step 5: Before Round 4, indicated that each group can send out a representative to meet with other group representatives for 3 minutes. Then conduct Rounds 4 through 6.

Step 6: Before Round 7, each group can again send out a representative to meet for 3 minutes. Then conduct Rounds 7 and 8.

Step 7: Before Round 9, indicate that there will be a 3 minute open forum and discussion period among participants.

Step 8: When the groups have completed Round 9, have participants total their scores.

Step 9: Conduct a large group discussion of the activities.

III. Reflection, Generalization, and Application

During debriefing use the following questions to generate discussion:

1. What is really the Community Dilemma?

2. What were the barriers you encountered as you played this game?

3. What were the factors which helped you during this game?

4. What were the leadership roles exhibited by various participants during this game?

5. What were your feelings as each round came and went?

6. How can you foster better communication among members of your small group and among members of the large group?

7. What are some principles learned?

Note: It's very important to emphasize that the purpose of this exercise is to greatly exaggerate the difference between competition and cooperation (win-lose versus win-win). However, a volatile atmosphere may be created and strong feelings may be expressed by participants during the activity. It is important that the facilitator allow adequate time for cooling down and venting of feelings during the debriefing period.

IV. Follow-up

Participants can be asked to identify instances of win-lose situations in their own work areas. It will be a challenge for them to turn the situation around so that it is a win-win for individuals, departments, the organization, and the community.

V. Activity

The information from the Directions and Small Group Score Sheet should be presented to participants. It can be spoken, written on a flip chart or chalkboard, or reproduced using a photocopier.

The Community Dilemma:
Directions and Small group Score Sheet

The object of Community Dilemma is to score the **maximum number of positive points**. Group scores will be posted where they are visible to all participants. Groups will have **three** minutes between rounds to decide which card (A or B) they wish to play.

Scoring for Community Dilemma is as follows:
> If all groups play an A card—than all groups receive +3 points.
> If a mixture of A and B cards are played—then groups playing an A card receive -6 points and groups playing a B card receive +6 points.
> If all groups play a B card—then all groups receive -3 points.

Round	Score	
1.	_____	
2.	_____	
3.	_____	Representatives from each group will have three minutes to meet after Round 3.
4.	_____	
5.	_____	
6.	_____	Scores are doubled for Round 6 and representatives from each group will have three minutes to meet after Round 6.
7.	_____	
8.	_____	There will be an open forum for discussion after Round 8.
9.	_____	Scores are doubled for Round 9.
Total	_____	

Community Dilemma:
Large Group Score Sheet

Groups

Rounds	1	2	3	4	5	6
1						
2						
3						

Representatives from each group meet

	1	2	3	4	5	6
4						
5						
6 Scores Doubled						

Representatives from each group meet

	1	2	3	4	5	6
7						
8						

Open forum for discussion

	1	2	3	4	5	6
9 Scores Doubled						
Total						

Comments, feelings expressed, and principles learned:

ACTIVITY 6.2
JOIN THE CLUB: COMMUNITY EXERCISE

I. Planning

Goal: Upon completing this activity, participants will be able to enhance their skills in collaboration and decision making.

Materials: Paper, pencils, and copies of the simulation activity.

Time: Approximately 1 hour to 90 minutes.

Size of Group: From 15 to 20 participants.

II. Involvement

Step 1: Explain that in this exercise the local school board is discussing a redefinition of its mission statement. Local clubs and organizations have been invited to a meeting to offer their input on tonight's topic: *What should be the school's philosophy of education?*

Step 2: Tell participants they must join one of the groups described in the activity. (If there are fewer than 3 participants per group, then one or more of the groups can be eliminated.)

Step 3: Indicate that each group has 30 minutes to (1) prepare/clarify a position on the issue and (2) develop a plan for its implementation to be presented at the school board meeting.

Step 4: Ask each group, in turn, to present its ideas. The group presentations should be short, no more than 5 to 10 minutes. Each group should select a spokesperson to represent the club's or organization's viewpoints and interests.

Step 5: After the small group presentations, conduct a discussion of the whole group to decide what philosophy should be adopted by the school.

III. Reflection, Generalization, and Application

During the group discussion, seek comments about effective communication and collaboration and how they relate to decision making in groups. Make the point that reaching consensus is difficult at times, especially when some participants have vested interests or strong viewpoints. Emphasize that the key to achieving consensus is through open communication, negotiation, and compromise, and that respect for diversity of opinions is an important quality as well.

IV. Follow-up

Diversity, opinions, and individual rights should be respected when dealing with others. Cooperation and collaboration, as well as effective communication skills, are excellent strategies to use when striving to make group decisions. Indicate that participants can begin to use these skills in meetings, one-on-one discussions, and even in phone and Internet interactions.

V. Activity

Each participant should be provided with a copy of the information sheet. This can be reproduced from the book.

JOIN THE CLUB: COMMUNITY EXERCISE

A town meeting has been called to deal with a proposal by the Federation of Religion and Culture to revise the curriculum in the local schools to promote moral education. The meeting has been well publicized and many members of the community plan to attend. The members of the community identify with one of the five groups named below. The ensuing discussion at the town meeting promises to be lively as each group vies to promote its ideas on how the school curriculum should be changed.

Members of each group should be prepared to present to the town meeting two issues: (1) a statement of their philosophical position on education and (2) a plan for a new school curriculum to reflect their position. After each group has presented its ideas, a general discussion should ensue to determine what changes in the school curriculum will be made.

The five groups are

1. The Home Life Society: Is interested in a better family life

2. Education Society: A volunteer organization for educational improvement, is committed to existing models of education

3. The Commerce Alliance: Lobbies for local business interests

4. The Federation of Religion and Culture: Is interested in spiritual and aesthetic enlightenment

5. The Children of Barbara Frietchie: Is committed to protect and defend the flag and that "for which it stands"

CHAPTER 7

Managing Volunteers: From Recruiting to Retaining

Try to imagine a city without civic or community leaders. Think of the social climate of a community that doesn't have Scout programs, services for seniors, child care centers, or counseling and rehabilitation programs for those who are in need. Suppose no one chose to volunteer. What would our world be like?

With today's uncertain political and economic environments, volunteerism and community leadership are needed desperately, especially in light of diminishing human, environmental, and financial resources. There is a strong need for volunteers to meet the human needs of our communities and to manage our society's resources.

"Historically, community education has included volunteers and promoted the notion of volunteer involvement. The Indiana state plan for community education professes the right citizens have to be involved in determining community needs, identifying community resources, and linking those needs and resources to improve their communities" (Wood, 1989, p. 3).

Many social and community agencies and other providers of human services expand or extend their services through the work of volunteers. In fact, some organizations would not be able to provide services at all without them. The former Indiana governor and secretary of health and human services, Dr. Otis Bowen, stated:

> Volunteerism represents a uniquely American tradition of citizen participation in community affairs. Indeed, our nation's history is replete with

examples of individual vigor and idealism mobilized within the structure of volunteer organizations and associations for the purpose of improving the quality of life within the American society. (Bowen & Kent, 1982)

WHY PEOPLE VOLUNTEER

Schindler-Rainman and Lippitt (1975) state that active volunteers come from primarily two paradigms: the self-actualizers and the servers. The authors indicate that "the self-actualizers see opportunities for learning, for excitement, for personal growth, while the servers see opportunities for significant contributions, for meeting needs and for action(s) relevant to improving society" (p. 50). It isn't that volunteers are from one extreme group or the other but rather that volunteers have differing priorities that affect why and where they volunteer and their commitment to the job.

A 1987 survey conducted by the National Volunteer Center revealed that the majority of people volunteer because of the desire to serve others, because they enjoy the work, or because they have an interest in the cause (cited in Murk & Stephan, 1994). Another survey in 1988 by the Gallup Organization revealed that volunteers reported that the reasons for volunteering were that they wanted to do something useful for someone else, they enjoyed the work, they had an interest in the activity or cause, or they wished to learn from the experience (Brudney, 1990). What this says about volunteers is that they are a diverse group with the dual expectations as described by Schindler-Rainman and Lippitt. Volunteers are looking for personal growth and a sense of satisfaction from serving others.

According to Hodgkinson and Weitzman (1996) in *Giving and Volunteering in the United States,* there are an estimated 98.4 million Americans (54.4 percent of adults 18 years of age or older) who volunteered an average of 4 hours per week in 1989. They gave a total of 20.5 billion hours. This total included 15.7 billion hours of formal volunteering (involving specific time commitments to organizations) and 4.8 billion hours of informal volunteering (helping neighbors or providing assistance on an ad hoc basis to organizations). The 15.7 billion hours of formal volunteering represented an estimated value of $170 billion. In addition, the estimated number of adults who volunteered increased 23 percent from 1987 to 1989.

Lynch (1984) discovered that people volunteer for many reasons other than helping other people. Although not listed in order of importance, the major reasons are as follows:

A. Good of Society

B. Socializing Skills
    1. To "get out of the house" or to escape boredom
    2. To make or meet new friends
    3. To be with old friends who volunteered for a program
    4. To gain knowledge about the problems of the community
    5. To spend "quality time" with members of their family by volunteering together

C. Personal Development Skills
    1. To make a transition from previous experience
    2. To maintain skills that they would otherwise no longer use

D. Employment Related Motives
    1. To get to know the important people in the community
    2. To gain new skills for a future paid position
    3. To impress their present employers for potential promotions within their companies
    4. To gain status or prestige by belonging to a special peer or business group

In summary, the primary reasons for volunteering are for the good of the community and society as well as for individual self-enhancement.

THE NEED FOR VOLUNTEERS

Volunteerism embodies a spirit of willingness (even eagerness) on the part of people to contribute their time, talents, and energies to a nonprofit organization without pay. There is often a strong willingness on the part of paid personnel to collaborate with volunteers on special projects.

The mission of a volunteer, according to Ilsley (1989), begins with a strong commitment to an agency or nonprofit organization, often without any type of binding agreement. This commitment may soon develop into a loyalty stronger than any written document. The volunteer does not think in terms of sacrifice but instead sees rewards that go beyond the financial gain. However, volunteers sacrifice much in terms of time spent and energies given to a project. Because of this, successful volunteer experience hinges on the mutual satisfaction of meeting volunteer and organizational needs.

Volunteers assume a wide variety of responsibilities in community organizations. They provide direct services to clients, they perform both clerical and administrative tasks, and they contribute their public relations, fund-raising, and grant-writing talents. Often they serve as leaders and policy makers by assuming roles and positions as board directors and technical advisers for special projects.

THE ROLES OF VOLUNTEERS

According to Ilsley (1989), "a volunteer is one who chooses to commit oneself to a cause or to others in a deliberate spirit of service, in response to one or more perceived social needs, within an organizational context, and in return for some psychic benefit" (p. 103).

Volunteers work in settings such as health, education, and religious organizations. They participate in social services, special action programs, recreation, arts and culture, business and political organizations. They assist the disabled, tutor illiterate students, raise funds for organizations, and assist with projects. They serve on boards and committees, participate in political campaigns, and lead recreational activities. They drive people from one place to another, answer phones, and stuff envelopes These are but a few examples of the myriad ways in which volunteers function in nonprofit programs which require their help to exist. Volunteers get involved for any number of reasons; however, unless an organization can guarantee their satisfaction through a positive work experience and through meaningful recognition, the volunteer will not likely remain active.

Many people volunteer because they benefit personally, not because they believe they can save humankind. This is not a selfish expression but rather a reflection of the saying: "Everyone needs to be needed." Volunteering often can bring new meaning to a person's life, new experiences, and a sense of being valued. Based on this knowledge, three suggestions are offered for identifying and recruiting volunteers:

1. Know your community (live there if possible). Get involved. Become an integral part of, and stakeholder in, the community.

2. Start with a list of volunteer prospects from interesting people you know. Broaden your circle of acquaintances by networking with other groups and people interested in youth or special projects such as churches, agencies, and concerned citizens.

3. Follow up with a telephone call or a personal visit in which you emphasize the benefits received and the important tasks or jobs to be performed. Be as specific as you can about the job description.

Smith (1981), a leading author in the field of volunteerism, states that many types of activities in which volunteers engage themselves may include

1. Service-oriented activities

2. Issue-oriented or cause-oriented activities

3. Activities for self-expression such as sport groups or dinner clubs

4. Activities for economic self-interest, such as professional groups and unions

5. Activities for philanthropic and fund-raising purposes

The first category described by Smith is service-oriented activities. Nonprofit agency directors can make extensive use of volunteers, asking them to fulfill a number of roles by giving them important responsibilities such as tutoring, counseling adults, involving them in staff development, training, problem solving, and decision making (for example, serving on boards and advisory councils).

Issue-oriented or cause-oriented activities, often called advocacy volunteerism, seek volunteers who will work to make community agencies and individuals aware of the need for social and community change. In both cases, volunteer commitment is based largely on a real sense of duty associated with improving life for one's fellow human beings, the community, and the environment. Dedicated participation also results in enriching one's own life.

GENERAL CONSIDERATIONS FOR WORKING WITH VOLUNTEERS

Brudney (1990) outlines a five-step approach to volunteer program design. The elements of an effective volunteer operation are (1) organizing the volunteer program, (2) matching volunteers and organizational needs, (3) educating volunteers for service, (4) training the organization's employees in volunteer management, and (5) evaluating and recognizing efforts.

Brudney suggests that any effort must have the administrative support necessary to run a volunteer program. Responsibilities such as recruitment, orientation, training, and evaluation cannot be taken lightly. There must be effective leadership and management directly responsible for the program. He also suggests that the structure of the organization be examined to evaluate the feasibility for volunteers to pursue their goals in conjunction with the regular paid employees of the organization.

Stone (1982) agrees with Brudney that adequate administration and leadership are a must. She recommends that

> A responsible agency will have definite, intelligent procedures for the
> selection and placement of its volunteers. Many agencies today are wise
> to have on staff a director of volunteers, a person responsible for initi-
> ating, planning, selecting, training and administrating the volunteer
> program. This includes recruiting, selecting, training, and assigning vol-
> unteers. (p. 6)

Organizations must search to find the right leadership
for volunteer coordination. The ideal person is committed to
the purpose and philosophy of the program and is someone
with the right personality and competencies to be effective.
Stenzel and Feeny (1976) suggest that the person must be willing
to devote the time to coordinate the effort, have vision, be objective, and possess the judgment and skill to evaluate the volunteers.

Richards (1979) recommends that the volunteer coordinator possess skills in consensus building and running meetings,
problem solving and decision making, long- and short-range
planning, interviewing, and skills in making public presentations (p. 9).

Effective volunteer programming depends upon the careful matching of volunteer skills and interests with the needs of
the organization. Brudney (1990) suggests that prior to recruiting volunteers, a survey of employees should be done to identify
possible tasks that might be best performed by volunteers. The
survey might also identify the willingness of employees to work
with volunteers. He also adds the importance of job descriptions
for volunteers that outline the essential requirements for the positions.

Overall, Brudney sees no difference in job description requirements for paid staff and volunteers. As for recruitment,
Brudney strongly suggests that every effort should be made to
interview and screen the applications for the positions, just as
a paid employee would be placed. The director and volunteer
program coordinators must develop an understanding of why

people become volunteers and what the organization has to offer. They must then devise a plan for matching the volunteers and the organization's needs.

RECRUITING, TRAINING, AND RETAINING VOLUNTEERS

Finding, educating, and keeping productive volunteers may be one of the most challenging tasks a director or agency coordinator can face. Finding the time, resources, and energy required to make the decision about whom to hire, train, and use is even more crucial to the success of the organization.

Recruiting Volunteers

Recruitment of volunteers should be done through a major campaign that addresses the needs of the agency, the needs of the volunteer, and the needs of the director. When recruiting volunteers it is helpful to present a job description to the applicant at the first meeting. The objectives should be specifically outlined as to the task, duration, duties, and meaning of the voluntary activity.

Before beginning a volunteer recruitment campaign, the volunteer director should prepare by assessing and implementing solid recruiting policies and practices. Talking with the new volunteers personally helps to ensure a high rate of success in recruiting personnel. Granted, personal interviews take more time, but volunteers are much less likely to respond to newspaper articles or advertisements than to personal contacts.

First, believe that volunteers are important to the success of the program. Believe that they can do the job effectively. Second, know exactly what jobs are needed for the volunteers to do, about how long each job will take, and how long the volunteers will help on the project. Third, help volunteers see that they can do the job, that the job is worthwhile, and that they are suited for the tasks outlined. Fourth, get them to commit themselves to the project and start the training right away. Sometimes, training doesn't begin with a formal meeting. Training may simply be observing another volunteer or group in action, reading important material or brochures about the program or project, or just talking in depth with another volunteer. However, for the best and most focused results, a formal training program for volunteers is recommended.

As part of the recruiting process, it is important to provide adequate information and sell the position. Be specific about the time and location. Six weeks of solid volunteer effort at one site is more effective than a long undetermined time at two or three locations. Break the job down into smaller components or manageable tasks. Be complimentary when asking a person to help. Don't apologize for asking someone to help you; that's like saying that you just couldn't find any else. Be positive in your approach. Ask someone who already knows how to do part of the job. People will usually volunteer to help with something familiar to them before they volunteer for a brand new task. Find two or more people to help with the same job. People tend to feel more comfortable is they have a friend or an associate to assist them do a job.

When training volunteers, never assume that they know everything they will need to know about the agency. Everyone needs a good orientation or training program. In order to design a meaningful volunteer training program, questions in three important areas should be raised:

1. What knowledge, skills, and abilities does a volunteer need to perform the assignment? Which require further training and orientation?

2. What kinds of skill does the program director or leader want this training session to produce? What are the manageable outcomes to be realized?

3. What kinds of individual learning experiences can be produced in the training sessions that will give a volunteer the

opportunity to practice and to develop those skills and perhaps reduce anxiety about the job?

Plambeck (1985), director of the National Academy of Volunteerism, suggests the following approaches for developing an effective training program.

1. Work with smaller groups. Smaller groups of 20 or 30 people allow opportunities to open up discussions and develop individual learning experiences. Also, small groups help to develop a sense of belonging.

2. Use volunteers from previous years as trainers, coaches, and mentors for the new volunteers. Experienced volunteers can be excellent in role-playing situations because they have heard and handled many of the problems and responsibilities. Mentors also lend credibility to a program or project—they have been there before.

3. Provide a self-scoring questionnaire on the facts about the agency. It can be a good ice-breaker and can motivate people to learn more about the agency. However, the questionnaire should be 20 items or less.

4. Allow time to role-play or use simulations where volunteers would be allowed to demonstrate new knowledge and practice skills in a "safe" atmosphere. Rotate roles with a participant observer as an interested spectator to provide observations after the session is concluded. New volunteers can receive feedback and coaching for a more effective performance after the session.

5. Divide the volunteers being trained into groups of six or seven and have them develop lists of problems they anticipate, questions for which they want answers, and potential difficulties. Prioritize the items on the lists and help the volunteers determine the appropriate answers. Previous volunteers can be used as good resources in the discussions and training sessions.

6. Work to increase the level of motivation throughout the session. Adult educator Wlodkowski (1986) indicates that teachers must pay attention to motivational needs from the inception of a program and throughout its duration, not just at the end of the learning experience.

Stenzel and Feeny (1976) describe a three-stage planning process for volunteer training. They emphasize that the content of training should flow from the needs and interests of those serving in relation to the objectives of the organization. This requires the director to first gather facts, which is accomplished by interviews, observations, or a review of current studies. They suggest the new volunteers as well as full-time paid staff be questioned to discover gaps in information or understanding. They also suggest monitoring patterns in the office that may lead to differences in opinions. Second, the information collected must be compiled. This involves evaluating what people know versus what they need to know. Third, they suggest identifying the framework for training.

Training Volunteers

One of the first items in training is deciding who should do the training. The trainer should be someone in a leadership position. This will help to ensure that the person has the knowledge to address questions. In addition, it will make an important impression having senior staff involved. By learning more about the preferred styles of the learners and their specific interests, the instruction can be delivered accordingly. Other topics to be considered are time, location, the learning needs of the volunteers, the skills of the instructor, and the amount and content of instruction. There must be adequate time for instruction at a time convenient for the volunteers.

The training location should be also designated with input for the volunteers. Transportation could be an issue. As much as possible, information should be gathered about the learning habits of the individuals. Some may prefer lecture, others discussion, and others role playing or group activity. These instructional methods and others are described in detail in *Adult Learning Methods* (Galbraith, 1998). All these factors will make training successful.

Understanding the ways adults learn also helps in developing meaningful, effective training programs. Important adult education principles, as described by Murk and Stephan (1994), are suggested for effective volunteer training:

- Adults have a strong desire to learn. Discover the formal and informal interests of the learners before the training begins.
- Adults will learn only when they feel a need to learn.
- Adults learn by doing, by practice, and by receiving constructive feedback, reinforcement, and direction.
- Using problem-solving skills and dealing with realistic situations work best for adults.
- Previous experience has a significant effect upon adult learning, and can be both positive and negative.
- Involve adults in informal and comfortable environments to foster learning.
- Use a variety of instructional methods when teaching adults.
- Use questioning strategies to stimulate, to recall factual information, to draw implications, and to make value judgments.
- Use spaced practice sessions to facilitate remembering skills or principles. Have the practices include both verbal and image rehearsals, depending on the nature of the task.
- Use descriptive feedback and reinforcement for participants. Compliment them specifically on tasks performed well rather than merely praising them for a "job well done."
- Use the "teachable moment" or significant event strategy for important learning and build important examples on relevant situations or real cases.
- Assist each participant in evaluating progress. Everyone likes to know how he or she is doing.
- Meet the social needs of the group. Use coffee breaks often. Schedule an outing or special occasion to celebrate the training completion.

• Adults want guidance, encouragement, and suggestions, not grades. The key to volunteers is not to "use them" but to utilize their important time, talents, and skills through meaningful training (pp. 18–20).

Retaining Volunteers

One of the most important aspects of retaining volunteers is to make them feel valued by the organization. If the volunteer's role is not perceived as being of value to the operation of the agency, the longevity of those services to the agency will be shortened. Activity 7.1, Volunteer Management Dilemma, and Activity 7.2, Making Cents: Conflict Resolution, will help readers gain insights into some of the issues related to keeping volunteers satisfied and on the job.

Retaining volunteers is dependent upon effectively managing them. As an effective manager of volunteers, one should consider the Dozen Principles of Managing People (Van Ness, 1992):

1. People will run farther than they can be driven.

2. People want to know that they are appreciated and acknowledged for efforts and performance. Reward and recognize often.

3. Let your people (volunteers) advance you as the manager/director and the organization by giving others credit often and well. When authorizing new things, emphasize that "You and I" are both accountable for consequences and results.

4. Focus on problems and alternative solutions, not fixing blame or punishment on the volunteer.

5. Use directives as the last resort. If directives are issued, let them result from an idea exchange.

6. Make solutions clear. Failure is often the result of not communicating or recognizing that a problem exists.

7. Focus on specifics, not generalities. Definitely do not admonish an individual volunteer in front of peers; consequently never admonish a group for individual failure. If you must make examples, choose good examples.

8. If you are trying to develop staff self-concepts or empower people, then tell volunteers what factors went into a decision.

9. Ask volunteer staff to help create a list of pros and cons for any action considered controversial or questionable. Consult technical or legal advisors if you think there may be a problem.

10. Include subordinates or volunteers in major decisions unless the situation prevents it or the decision is too controversial.

11. Approach volunteers as a group more capable than demands of the present position.

12. Treat all volunteers and staff as people on the way up. You'll gain the respect of others and get their help and assistance when you need it the most.

Another important aspect of retaining volunteers is to reward them for their contributions to the organization. Brudney presents evaluation of volunteers as a way to increase the volunteers' effectiveness, but more importantly he sees it as a means to compliment them. Because volunteers are driven by forces other than a paycheck, feedback about how the needs of both the volunteer and the organization are being met can serve as rewards. The extent to which the two (individual and organizational) needs are being met may also lead to additional tasks or other changes in positions, such as promotions or more responsibility.

Recognition can be accomplished in a variety of ways. Award ceremonies, newspaper articles, photos, certificates, and personal gratitude are among the types of rewards Brudney (1990) recommends (pp. 115–116). Regular monthly meetings in which volunteers and staff can confer, monthly newsletters with pictures that highlight the activities of volunteers, and other means of communication are extremely valuable. Much of this value accrues when volunteers are included in regular in-service meetings, seminars, and workshops designed for the paid staff. Certainly, a sense of belonging or affiliation can be fostered, which further serves to solidify the volunteer workers' resolve and reaffirms their value as part of the staff. Recognition nights, posters, pins, pictures, letters of support and appreciation, and constructive suggestions help to emphasize the role of the volunteer as an important and integral part of the agency or organization. Resources like volunteers are scarce, valuable, and limited and should be treated as such.

It is best to utilize the volunteers' time, talents, and skills wisely. Through careful planning, effective recruiting, ongoing training, and adequate recognition, volunteers can realize their full potential. Treat volunteers in the same way as paid staff and reward them often.

SUMMARY

A sign of a well-managed volunteer agency is when people see themselves and others as capable of significant personal development, when relationships are honest and supportive, when risk is accepted as a condition for growth and change, when there is trust and mutual respect, and when the volunteer director and others admit their mistakes and learn from them. Good volunteer management inspires people and empowers agency personnel. This can be accomplished through solid management practices and positive approaches to making volunteers and non-profit agencies more productive and responsible. Volunteers are a community's greatest resource—and an important part of its future.

The exercises which follow are designed to heighten awareness of the issues of working with volunteers. Activity 7.1, Volunteer Management Dilemma, shows that there may be difficult issues to address. Every volunteer may present different issues, each of which needs to be dealt with. Activity 7.2, Making Cents: Conflict Resolution, is another exercise in resolving potential and actual conflicts with and among volunteers. These activities are designed to help those who manage and work with volunteers appreciate them as people committed to making a change as well as dedicated workers.

ACTIVITY 7.1
VOLUNTEER MANAGEMENT DILEMMA

I. Planning

Goal: Upon completing this activity, participants will be able to identify and discuss the philosophical and practical dilemmas of operating a volunteer program.

Materials: Paper, pencils, and copies of the activity.

Time: 45 to 60 minutes.

Size of Group: From 3 to 5 members in each group, and a total of up to 20 participants.

II. Involvement

Step 1: Provide a copy of the activity to participants and ask them to read it.

Step 2: Indicate that each group will have 30 minutes to create a plan for resolving the dilemma by responding to the discussion questions at the end.

Step 3: After 30 minutes have elapsed, or when everyone has completed the exercise, ask for volunteers to share their solutions.

III. Reflection, Generalization, and Application

Encourage discussion with the entire group. Explain that no matter how well we plan, unforeseen events and challenges arise every day. Seek responses or make the learning point that the greatest resource for managing dilemmas comes in the form of people. In the exercise and on the job, empowering others is one way to get the job done while at the same time increasing worker satisfaction and self-worth.

IV. Follow-up

Ask participants to identify volunteer issues where they work and explore possible solutions to problems. Sharing ideas among participants may generate useable solutions.

V. Activity

Each participant should be provided with a copy of the Volunteer Management Dilemma.

VOLUNTEER MANAGEMENT DILEMMA

You are the director of a medium-sized community service, nonprofit agency. You have a staff of 6 professionals and also use a total of 35 volunteers who contribute more than 150 hours each week.

Recently, the newspaper from your city published an editorial that applauded the work of your agency, especially its outreach program, and encouraged significant expansion of your service area. At the same time, however, your major funding source (United Way) announced a 10 percent budget reduction for the coming year.

To make matters worse, the following major events occurred this past week:

- The two most active and influential volunteers have claimed they are dissatisfied and are considering leaving.

- The staff member responsible for coordinating and supervising the volunteers sent you a memo that said due to health problems, she must resign effective Friday of this week.

Discussion Questions

1. What types of information would you like and actually need to begin working toward a solution to the dilemma?
2. What are your alternatives (internal and external)?
3. How would you resolve this dilemma?

ACTIVITY 7.2
MAKING CENTS: CONFLICT RESOLUTION

I. Planning

Goal: Upon completing this activity, participants will be better able to resolve conflicts in a way that benefits all parties.

Materials: Copies of role-playing information for each participant.

Time: 10 minutes.

Size of Group: 2 or 3 people per exercise (see options under II. Involvement).

II. Involvement

This activity can be conducted in three different ways: Fishbowl, Pairs, and Triads. The directions for each format are outlined below.

A. Fishbowl

Step 1: Select two participants to role-play in front of the entire group. (You may want to choose people who are comfortable speaking in front of an audience.)

Step 2: Assign one role to each of the two participants and give them a few minutes to read their roles and prepare for the role play.

Step 3: Ask the two participants to sit or stand where they can be seen and heard by all members of the group. Then instruct them to begin the role play.

Step 4: Stop the role play when the situation is resolved or when the role play has ceased to be productive.

Step 5: Ask the two participants to express their feelings regarding the experience.

Step 6: Ask the other members of the group to offer comments about what transpired during the role play.

B. Pairs

Step 1: Divide the group into pairs.

Step 2: Hand out the roles and ask one person in each pair to assume the role of supervisor and the other person to assume the role of associate.

Step 3: Give the participants a few minutes to familiarize themselves with their roles and to prepare for the role play.

Step 4: Instruct the participants to begin the role play activity. Observe the interaction and stop the activity when the situation has been resolved or the discussion is no longer productive.

Step 5: Ask participants to comment on what happened in their pairs.

C. Triads

Step 1: Divide the group into triads, or groups of three.

Step 2: Hand out the roles and ask one person in each triad to assume the role of supervisor, another person to assume the role of associate, and a third person should be the observer.

Step 3: Give the participants a few minutes to familiarize themselves with their roles and to prepare for the role play.

Step 4: Instruct the participants to begin the role play activity. Observe the interaction and stop the activity when the situation has been resolved or the discussion is no longer productive.

Step 5: The observer should provide feedback to the role players regarding the interaction and what feelings were observed.

Step 6: Conduct a whole group discussion to share thoughts and identify the dynamics of the role play activity.

III. Reflection, Generalization, and Application

Conflict is as much a part of everyday life as going to work. It is how we handle conflict that often determines our degree of success, teamwork, and overall work satisfaction. By realizing that conflict situations are going to arise, and that disagreements aren't necessarily bad, people can begin to work toward acceptable solutions and not focus on their lack of agreement. In fact, conflict situations, when handled effectively, can lead to new and innovative ways of addressing problems and challenges.

IV. Follow-up

Participants now have a better understanding of how conflict comes about and what to do when confronted with a potentially difficult situation. By using skills such as empathy, listening, and a solution-oriented approach, they can turn a loss into a win for everyone involved.

V. Activity

The information for the participants can be spoken, written on a flip chart or chalkboard, or reproduced from this book using a photocopier.

MAKING CENTS: CONFLICT RESOLUTION

Supervisor Information

You supervise a group of volunteers who work at an agency in a rural setting. As part of their job, some volunteers drive to and from clients' homes. Agency guidelines on gas reimbursement allow for $0.30 per mile, which you believe is fair, especially with the number of economy cars on the road.

One of the volunteers, who lives some distance from the agency, has asked to speak with you about mileage reimbursement. You suspect this person may be seeking an increase in the reimbursement amount.

You are open to suggestions, but you know the person drives a compact car that can be easily operated for $0.30 a mile. You'll just have to play it by ear.

Associate Information

You are a volunteer at an agency that is 25 miles from your home. In addition, you have to drive to and from clients' homes as part of your job.

You like helping others and enjoy the rural setting of the agency. However, the recent increase in gas prices is making your driving more costly.

The current reimbursement policy at the agency is $0.30 per mile. You would like to see the amount increased, possibly to $0.35, because you believe you cannot continue to operate your car for only $0.30 per mile.

CHAPTER 8

Continuing Professional and Organizational Development

The quest for ongoing improvement in nonprofit and volunteer organizations is tantamount to the success of agencies, community programs, and charitable efforts small and large. Both individuals and organizations have many opportunities and challenges to be more efficient, effective, and productive while, at the same time, managing streamlined budgets and resources.

This book presents numerous ways to work with people to provide the best service possible for those in need. Exercises, techniques, and simulations are only part of the solution, however. Transferring those newly learned skills and behaviors back to the job is what really counts. Without a plan of action and some degree of implementation, even the best ideas won't make much of a difference.

BUILDING BLOCKS OF AN EFFECTIVE ADULT AND COMMUNITY EDUCATOR

Adult and community educators constantly strive for improvement. Often professional development makes us aware of knowledge and skills that we lack and need to acquire to be more competent in our jobs. What can be overlooked, however, are other areas of equal importance. Figure 8.1 illustrates the essential components required for adult and community educators to be effective on their jobs. The model consists of three

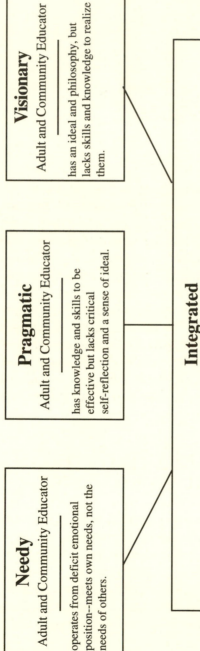

Needy
Adult and Community Educator

operates from deficit emotional position--meets own needs, not the needs of others.

Pragmatic
Adult and Community Educator

has knowledge and skills to be effective but lacks critical self-reflection and a sense of ideal.

Visionary
Adult and Community Educator

has an ideal and philosophy, but lacks skills and knowledge to realize them.

Integrated
Adult and Community Educator

• Affective or Emotional Qualities: Has a positive affect including awareness of own strengths and weaknesses; has ability to meet the needs of others, not self; does not let situational stress affect relationships with learners or colleagues; and does not exhibit other behaviors which detract from effectiveness.

• Knowledge and Skills: Has knowledge and skills regarding adult learners, organization and community context, and subject matter; possesses process and interpersonal skills; and knows techniques for teaching, learning, program planning, negotiating, leading and managing, and budgeting.

• Philosophy and Ethics: Engages in self-reflection; understands the various philosophical orientations; has a well-developed sense of ideal; and has a personal code of ethics.

Figure 8.1 Building blocks of an effective adult and community educator (Dean, 1997)

broad areas: affective or emotional qualities, knowledge and skills, and philosophy and ethics. Each area has its strengths and weaknesses. Combining these areas through professional development creates effectiveness.

First, adult educators need to be aware of their affective or emotional side and how this impacts their functioning on the job. This area is often overlooked in lists of the requisites for success in adult and community education. The affective area consists of several components. Foremost is an awareness of personal strengths and weaknesses and the ability to compensate for the weaknesses. In addition, adult and community educators must meet the needs of others as opposed to meeting their own needs. Unfortunately, we can all think of leaders who are a detriment to their clients, organizations, and communities because they are so busy meeting their own emotional needs that they are not even aware that they are not meeting the needs of others. Examples include people who so want approval that they cannot say "no" to others, even when that is the appropriate response, or people who need to feel important and use their job to increase their status rather than actually help others. Another component in the affective area is the ability to continue focusing on the job and the clients regardless of day-to-day situational stresses. We all have bad days, but the ability to not let those negative forces interfere with how we treat others is critical to success on the job. Lastly, adult and community educators should be free from other behaviors that would detract from their ability to get along with others or perform their jobs.

The second major area encompasses the knowledge and skills required of effective adult and community educators. These are the topics most often addressed in lists of effective behaviors. They include (but are not limited to) knowledge and skills regarding the adult learners or clients; the organization and community contexts; subject matter or topics addressed in the programs; and process skills and knowledge such as interpersonal skills, teaching techniques, program planning, negotiating, leading and managing, and budgeting.

The third major area needing attention is the philosophical basis from which the adult and community educator operates.

As has been pointed out more than once (Beder, 1989; Elias & Merriam, 1995; Merriam & Brockett, 1997) a person's philosophies have a direct impact on professional behavior, even if the philosophical basis is not clearly articulated. The ability to engage in critical reflection to define personal beliefs is one of the most important aspects of professional development. The following qualities are direct outgrowths of appropriate self-critical reflection. A knowledge of philosophical orientation is important in order to be able to define a philosophical position. In addition, a well-developed sense of what we believe is the ideal will help us define and choose appropriate behaviors in different situations. This "sense of ideal" may be as broad as an image of what the world should look like or as specific as defining learner-teacher interaction. Closely tied to a philosophical orientation and a sense of ideal is a personal code of ethics. This code does not need to be formal or prescribed by an organization or professional association. However, it needs to be a well-developed statement of what we as adult and community educators believe is the right thing to do in various circumstances.

What happens when adult and community educators have not spent the time and energy in developing in all of these areas? Several scenarios can be identified. First we might find the "needy" adult and community educator. This is a person who operates primarily from meeting personal needs on the job, rather than the needs of others. Second is the "pragmatic" adult and community educator. Pragmatic people focus on the knowledge and skills to be successful without giving much attention to why they are doing what they are doing. They may be very accomplished or skillful, but do not have a sense of the big picture or ideal that drives the best professionals in the field. Third is the "visionary" adult and community educator. This type of person has an ideal, but has not developed the knowledge and skills to be able to realize the ideal. Often such people are well-intentioned but ineffective in their actions. An "integrated" adult and community educator is one who has healthy affective qualities, is well versed in the knowledge and skills required to do the job, and also has a well-developed sense of the ideal and philosophical bases. These people can function at all levels and are aware when they are not doing well or need help, as well as when to offer assistance to others.

The key element in professional development is the routine practice of critical reflection which enables an educator to identify personal strengths and weaknesses as well as to develop a plan for building on strengths and compensating for weaknesses. No one expects to be perfect, nor do we expect others to be perfect. Engaging in critical self-reflection can be aided by using the experiential learning activities in this book. The activities will help professionals think through their current practice and develop future practice.

ASSESSING STRENGTHS AND WEAKNESSES

Before a plan can be put into action, it is important to survey employee strengths and weaknesses. Who is the best person for the job? What qualifications are needed to ensure success? What are the personal and organizational benefits? Answering these questions will allow improvement programs to meet an individual's needs while effectively tending to the larger needs of the organization.

It is easy for many leaders and managers to recognize an individual's strengths and weaknesses. The question is, how can this information be useful? One problem is that some leaders may take for granted that a strength will be used effectively and appropriately by a person. In this case some coaching may well help a person make full use of personal assets. Another problem arises if weaknesses are viewed as deficits instead of opportunities for growth and development. With this in mind, here is a list of areas where individual qualities, whether viewed as strengths or weaknesses, may play a role in advancing the organization's plan.

- **Special attitudes or resources:** Mechanical ability, a green thumb, sales ability, or skill in building or repairing things
- **Intellectual qualities:** Curiosity and an ability to learn and en-

joy learning; thinking out ideas and expressing them aloud or in writing

- **Education, training, instruction:** Secondary education, advanced study, vocational training, on-the-job training, special courses, and self-instruction; high grades and scholastic honors
- **Work, vocation, job, or positions:** Experience in a particular field or various positions; management or self-employment; relations with coworkers; job satisfaction, pride, and loyalty to organization
- **Aesthetics:** Unique interests or recognition in the arts, ability to express oneself, and other intangibles.
- **Organization skills:** Leadership positions, ability to develop goals, organize work, and prioritize
- **Hobbies and crafts:** Interests or avocations including instruction or training
- **Expressive arts:** Dancing, sketching, painting, sculpture, pottery, and music, to name a few
- **Health:** Preventive measures to ensure health, including checkups, timely treatment, diet, and exercise
- **Sports and outdoor activities:** Participation in organized athletics, camping, biking, hiking, and regular exercise
- **Creativity:** Sense of play and imagination at home, with family, on the job or avocation
- **Personal relations:** Ability to meet and talk freely with people; be polite, respectful, and aware of other's feelings; listen and attend to person's needs; empathize and help others regardless of sex, creed, race, or nationality
- **Emotion:** Ability to give as well as receive affection or love; feel and/or express a wide range of emotions; empathize by putting self in other's shoes; understand role of emotions in everyday life; sense of humor

Other positive qualities include risk taking, tenacity, knowledge of foreign languages or cultures, public speaking, and a sense of adventure.

Not everyone will excel in all these areas, of course, but by capitalizing on an individual's strengths and growth areas, the work group will become more productive and effective. This leads to more goals being met, greater worker satisfaction, and personal and professional development.

ACHIEVEMENT THROUGH MOTIVATION

The objective of any leader or manager is to enable others to take positive actions in selecting and accomplishing goals. One of the most important steps in that process is enhancing each individual's self-concept to ensure success. By providing an increased sense of self-worth in others, a leader creates a group of energized, motivated people who will seek new and challenging activities.

Every person experiences three basic motivations and how well these motivators are addressed is directly related to an individual's sense of value and satisfaction to the organization. Almost everyone gets some gratification from being helpful to others. Others get satisfaction from "making a difference" and being valued as a helping person. Yet others are motivated by taking initiative and getting others to accomplish goals. It is important to understand that everyone is motivated by different—but no less important—goals and desires for helping. Only then can organizational goals be matched with individual motivations, which sets the stage for a win-win situation.

DEVELOPING A CAN-DO ATTITUDE

Negativism in our contemporary society has a direct impact on our potential or, rather, our lack of potential. In addition, economic uncertainty and instability have created a work environment where it has become fashionable to "eliminate weaknesses," "trim the fat," and "diminish shortcomings" within organizations. There is no question that constructive criticism has played, and will continue to play, a role in positive growth and learning with individuals and within organizations. Performance evaluations and day-to-day supervision, however, are sometimes anything but constructive. The result can be a negative working environment in which employee motivation is diminished or even destroyed.

For leaders and influential people to motivate others to achieve organizational goals, they must firmly believe that every person possesses unlimited potential. This potential can be tapped and used effectively by responding to each person in ways that build self-image. When given adequate support and confidence, a person will be willing to take risks and grow in the position—and as an individual—which benefits the organization. This concept of "I can" is based on the premise that being positive and reinforcing, rather than pointing out failures, can expand people's potential.

If leaders in the adult and community education begin to focus on meaningful and productive goal setting, involving an affirming attitude about themselves and others, the potential of workers and volunteers can be turned into results. This means higher worker satisfaction, expanded collaboration, and enhanced productivity in the organization—and better opportunities and services for people in need.

MAKING THE TIME

With so much time devoted to managing daily operations and handling crises, it is often difficult to plan for organizational and professional development. It takes commitment and courage to make professional development an organizational priority. Yet without it the organization's effectiveness may be diminished or even cease to exist. The most successful organizations factor in time and money to ensure their people are growing and becoming more productive in helping achieve organizational goals. But with limited resources and budgets, how is this possible?

Taking time to listen to workers is often an inexpensive way to uncover solutions. This can be done through periodic updates and brainstorming meetings, or even casual hallway conversations. Using employees' ideas is also a good way to build their self-esteem and gain commitment to moving the organization forward. Utilizing people's attributes, such as their teaching or training experience, is another way to help workers achieve their potential and have their expertise acknowledged. It's also possible to observe other organizations to determine what they are doing right and, possibly more important, what they are no longer doing because it was counterproductive to organizational goals.

Is it possible to devote so much time and resources to professional development and still meet organizational goals? Currently Harley-Davidson Motor Cycle Company devotes about 80 hours of training and professional development time per employee per year and its productivity has continued to increase (Rhonda White, personal communication, February 6, 1998). Professional development does not take people off the job and decrease productivity—it makes people so much more motivated and effective on the job that their productivity will increase.

PUTTING A PLAN IN ACTION

Probably the most formidable task for any director or manager is making the changes needed to become a more successful organization. People are generally resistant to change and may not wish to abandon the status quo. Therefore, it is important for organizational leaders to work side by side with employees and volunteers as the plan for improvement begins to unfold. Gaining commitment and buy-in through collaboration and teamwork will go a long way toward ensuring the success of any implementation.

One way to help sell the program and any major changes is to get the word out and be willing to listen to feedback. People are usually fair and supportive when they are involved in the decision making. By developing a sense of cooperation and a willingness to compromise, the organizational leaders will garner support and commitment that is often missing when mandates are handed down from management.

Involving others in scheduling training and improvement programs also shows that their opinions and ideas are valued, the assumption being that they in turn will work with the organization toward enhancing processes, policies, and the environment.

SUMMARY

It is no secret that nonprofit and volunteer organizations must improve how they function and manage resources if they are going to continue operating. There are ways, however, to make organizations and the people who work there more productive, satisfied, and customer-oriented. The business world contains numerous examples of top-notch organizations, such as WalMart, Apple Computers, and Edy's Grand Ice Cream, to name a few, that have dedicated themselves to ongoing professional and organizational improvement.

The same can be said for organizations in adult and community education. Making a continuous effort to improve services—both internal and external—while committing to staff development is the key to success. Those organizations that take the time now to invest in their people will reap rewards in the future; those that don't may find themselves out of business.

The activity that follows, Activity 8.1, Professional Development Plan, is designed to help adult and community educators clarify their professional development concerns and goals. The activity will help foster critical reflection through the use of a "force-field" analysis of professional development goals.

The major premise of this book is that professional and organizational development are not independent activities. Indeed, many people see them as competing activities—each potentially taking valuable resources away from the other. In fact, they can and should be interrelated processes that mutually support one another. Professional development focuses on individuals; organizational development on the collective. The combination of these processes allows for individual development within a framework that promotes the organization's goals.

ACTIVITY 8.1
PROFESSIONAL DEVELOPMENT PLAN

I. Planning

Goal: After completing this activity, participants will be able to identify professional development goals, the resources needed to reach their goals, time frames for reaching goals, and forces that may facilitate or hinder their success.

Materials: Pencils, paper, and copies of the two worksheets.

Time: 30 minutes to 1 hour.

Size of group: Any number of people.

II. Involvement

Step 1: Discuss with the participants the concepts that personal growth, professional development, and organizational development are often intertwined and can complement one another. Emphasize that weaknesses are not necessarily negative and that they may provide opportunities for growth, such as additional training, computerized instruction, or more responsibilities on the job.

Step 2: Ask participants to use the Professional Development Plan Worksheet to list as many examples under each heading as possible. Participants are to list areas in which they feel they need additional skills or knowledge, the resources they feel they will need to acquire those skills and knowledge, and the time frame that they feel is reasonable for them to acquire the skills and knowledge. Participants may find it useful to work in small groups of two or three. This will help them brainstorm and critique ideas.

Step 3: Individually or in small groups, participants should use the Professional Development Force-Field Analysis to list the facilitators and the barriers to each of their professional development goals. This will help participants to identify support systems that are either in place or that can be developed as well as to anticipate barriers before they arise. The goal for the worksheet may be derived from the skills/knowledge section of the Professional Development Plan Worksheet.

III. Reflection Generalization, and Application

One of the most effective ways to realize goals—both personal and professional—is to write them down. The same goes for developmental plans. By creating a "concrete" plan in writing, individuals are more likely to be committed to following through and realizing their dreams.

IV. Follow-up

Indicate that this exercise will help the individual and the organization and, in the long run, will make people's jobs more satisfying and rewarding. Participants should keep copies of their professional development plans for future reference.

V. Activity

You may want to make multiple copies the Professional Development Plan Worksheet and the Professional Development Force-Field Analysis for each participant.

Professional Development Plan Worksheet		
Skills/Knowledge Areas Needing Improvement	Resources How will you acquire the skill/knowledge?	Time Frame When will you acquire the skill/knowledge?

Professional Development Force-Field Analysis

Goal: _____

Steps Needed to Reach Goal	Facilitators Forces Helping Me Reach Goal	Barriers Forces Keeping Me from Reaching Goal

REFERENCES

Apps, J. W. (1989). Providers of adult and continuing education: A framework. In S. B. Merriam & P. M. Cunningham (Eds.), *Handbook of adult and continuing education* (pp. 275–286). San Francisco: Jossey-Bass.

Arrow, K. J., Mnookin, R. H., Ross, L., Tversky, A., & Wilson, R. B. (1985). *Barriers to conflict resolution*. New York: W. W. Norton & Co.

Aycox, F. (1985). *Games we should play in school*. Byron, CA: Front Row Experience.

Bass, B. M. (1990). From transactional to transformational leadership: Learning to share the vision. *Organizational Dynamics, 18*(3), 19–21.

Bass, B. M., & Avolio, B. J. (Eds.). (1994). *Improving organizational effectiveness through transformational leadership*. Thousand Oaks, CA: Sage.

Beder, H. (1989). Purposes and philosophies of adult education. In S. B. Merriam & P. M. Cunningham (Eds.), *Handbook of adult and continuing education* (pp. 37–50). San Francisco: Jossey-Bass.

Bennis, W. G. (1989). *On becoming a leader*. Reading, MA: Addison Wesley Publishing Company.

Bergevin, P. A. (1967). *A philosophy for adult education*. New York: Seabury Press.

Biddle, W., & Biddle, L. (1965). *The community development process: The rediscovery of local initiative*. New York: Holt, Rinehart, and Winston.

Blake, R., & Mouton, J. S. (1964). *The managerial grid*. Houston, TX: Gulf.

Blanchard, K. (1990, January). *Principles of effective leadership*. Presentation given at Johnstown Area Vocational School, Johnstown, PA.

Blau, R., & Scott, R. (1962). *Formal organizations: A comparative approach*. San Francisco: Chandler.

Bolt, J. F. (1989). *Executive development: A strategy for corporate competitiveness.* New York: Harper & Row.

Borman, E. G. (1969). *Discussion and group methods: Theory and Practice.* New York: Harper & Row.

Bowen, O. R., & Kent, G. (1982). *A manual for volunteer program development.* (Published through ACTION Grant # 437-5012/2 & Lilly Endowment, Inc.). The Governor's Voluntary Action Program, Room 117 State House, Indianapolis, IN.

Brockett, R. (1989). Professional associations for adult and continuing education. In S. B. Merriam & P. M. Cunningham (Eds.), *Handbook of adult and continuing education* (pp. 112–123). San Francisco: Jossey-Bass.

Brudney, J. L. (1990). *Fostering volunteer programs in the public sector: Planning, initiating and managing voluntary activities.* San Francisco: Jossey-Bass.

Brunner, C. (1991). *Thinking collaboratively: Ten questions and answers to help policy makers improve children's services.* Washington, DC: Education and Human Services Consortium, Institute for Educational Leadership.

Burns, J. M. (1978). *Leadership.* New York: Harper & Row.

Byrne, J. A., Brandt, J., & Port, O. (1993, February 8). The virtual corporation. *Business Week, 18,* 98–102.

Caffarella, R. S. (1994). *Planning programs for adult learners: A practical guide for educators, trainers, and staff developers.* San Francisco: Jossey-Bass.

Cardoza, G. (1996). *Higher education, scientific research and sustainable development in Latin America. Elements for a new agenda.* A paper presented at Harvard University Conference on The Americas, Cambridge, MA.

Cervero, R. M., & Wilson, A. L. (1994). *Planning responsibly for adult education: A guide to negotiating power and interests.* San Francisco: Jossey-Bass.

Cohen, W. A. (1990). *The art of the leader.* Englewood Cliffs, NJ: Prentice Hall.

Collins, M. (1991). *Adult education as vocation: A critical role for the adult educator.* New York: Routledge.

Cookson, P. S. (Ed.). (1998). *Program planning for the training and continuing education of adults: North American perspectives.* Malabar, FL: Krieger.

Dean, G. J. (1993a, November). *A process model of experiential learning in adult education.* Paper presented at the National Conference of the American Association for Adult and Continuing Education, Dallas, TX.

Dean, G. J. (1993b). Community education: A conceptual framework. In D. Flannery (Ed.), *Proceedings of the 34th Annual Adult Education Research Conference, 1993* (pp. 107–112). State College, PA: The Pennsylvania State University.

Dean, G. J. (1994a). Community and adult education: A conceptual framework for theory and practice. In G. Dean & T. Ferro (Eds.), *Proceedings of the Pennsylvania Adult and Continuing Education Research Conference, 1994* (pp. 3–10). Indiana, PA: Indiana University of Pennsylvania.

Dean, G. J. (1994b). *Designing instruction for adult learners.* Malabar, FL: Krieger.

Dean, G. J. (1997). Reflective practice for professional development. Workshop presented at the 1997 National Conference on Mentoring, Supervision, and Training, Pittsburgh, PA.

Dean, G. J. (1998). The six key tasks of leaders in adult and community education. Unpublished manuscript, Indiana University of Pennsylvania, Indiana, PA.

Dean, G. J., & Dowling, W. (1987). Community development: An adult education model. *Adult Education Quarterly, 37*(2), 78–89.

de Tocqueville, A. (1981). *Democracy in America.* New York: Modern Library.

Dewey, J. (1938). *Experience and education.* New York: Macmillan.

Draves, W. (1984). *How to teach adults.* Manhattan, KS: The Learning Resources Network.

Drucker, P. F. (1967). *The effective executive.* New York: Harper & Row.

Drucker, P. F. (1990). *Managing the nonprofit organization: Practice and principles.* New York: Harper Collins.

Elias, J. L., & Merriam, S. B. (1995). *Philosophical foundations of adult education* (2nd ed.). Malabar, FL: Krieger.

Esterby-Smith, M. (1987). Change and innovation in higher education: A role for corporate strategy? *Higher Education, 16,* 37–52.

French, W. (1964). *The personnel management process.* Boston, MA: Houghton-Mifflin Company, 536–38.

Gagne, R. M., Briggs, L. J., & Wager, W. W. (1988). *Principles of instructional design* (3rd ed.). Fort Worth, TX: Holt, Rinehart, and Winston.

Galbraith, M. W. (Ed.). (1998). *Adult learning methods: A guide for effective instruction* (2nd ed.). Malabar, FL: Krieger.

Galbraith, M. W., & Zelenak, B. (1989). The education of adult and continuing education practitioners. In S. B. Merriam & P. M. Cunningham (Eds.), *Handbook of adult and continuing education* (pp. 124–133). San Francisco: Jossey-Bass.

Galbraith, M. W., Sisco, B. R., & Guglielmino, L. M. (1997). *Administering successful programs for adults: Promoting excellence in adult, community, and continuing education.* Malabar, FL: Krieger.

Groff, W. H. (1980). *Key external data required in strategic decision making: A new role for management systems.* Opinion Paper. (ERIC Document Reproduction Service No. ED 201 295).

Hamilton, E., & Cunningham, P. M. (1989). Community based adult education. In S. B. Merriam & P. M. Cunningham (Eds.), *Handbook of adult and continuing education* (pp. 439–450). San Francisco: Jossey-Bass.

Handy, T. J. (1990, November). *The necessity of environmental scanning prior to long-range planning activities at high education institutions.* Paper presented at the Conference of the Mid-South Educational Research Association, New Orleans, LA. (ERIC Document Reproduction Service No. ED 326 156).

Hearn, J. C., & Heydinger, R. B. (1985). Scanning the university's external environment: Objectives, constraints, and possibilities. *Journal of Higher Education, 56,* 419–445.

Hersey, P., & Blanchard, K. H. (1988). *Management of organizational behavior: Utilizing human resources* (5th Ed.). Englewood Cliffs, NJ: Prentice-Hall.

Hodgkinson, V. A., & Weitzman, M. S. (1996). *Giving and volunteering in the United States: Findings from a national survey.* Washington, DC: The Independent Sector.

Houle, C. O. (1972). *The design of education.* San Francisco: Jossey-Bass.

Ilsley, P. J. (1989). The voluntary sector and adult education. In S. B. Merriam & P. Cunningham (Eds.), *The handbook of adult and continuing education* (pp. 99–111). San Francisco: Jossey-Bass.

Imel, S., & Sandoval, G. T. (1990). *Ohio at-risk linkage team project.* (A report on three state team projects). Columbus, OH: The Ohio State University, The Center for Education and Training for Employment.

Janove, E. B. (1984). *A methodology: The cyclic process.* Muncie, IN: Ball State University, The Institute for Community Education Development.

Katz, I. (1991, March 4). Breaking new ground: A strategic plan for United Way of Central Indiana, 1991–94. *Indianapolis Star,* p. C4.

Kelly, F. J. (1991). Evolution in leadership in American higher education: A changing paradigm. *Journal for Higher Education Management*, 7(1), 29–34.

Knowles, M. S. (1980). *The modern practice of adult education: From
pedagogy to andragogy*. New York: Association Press.

Knox, A. B. (1986). *Helping adults learn: A guide to planning, implementing, and conducting programs*. San Francisco: Jossey-Bass.

Kolb, D. A. (1984). *Experiential learning: Experience as the source of
learning and development*. Englewood Cliffs, NJ: Prentice-Hall.

Koontz, H., O'Donnell, C., & Weihrich, H. (1986). *Essentials of management* (4th ed.). New York: McGraw-Hill.

Kotter, J. P. (1990). *A force for change: How leadership differs from
management*. New York: Free Press.

Kotter, J. P. (1991). What leaders really do. *Harvard Business Review*.
68(3), pp. 3–11.

Kouzes, J. M., & Posner, B. Z. (1987). *The leadership challenge: How
to get extraordinary things done in organizations*. San Francisco:
Jossey-Bass.

Kowalski, T. J. (1988). *The organization and planning of adult education*. Albany, NY: SUNY Press.

Lauffer, A. (1978). *Doing continuing education and staff development*.
New York: McGraw-Hill.

Lee, M. (1989). Learning leadership. *Leadership Abstracts*, 2(1), 21.

Lowry, P. S. (1995). *Identifying and analyzing sponsors*. The Faculty
Research Handbook, 1995–96. Muncie, IN: Ball State University,
The Office of Academic Research and Sponsored Programs.

Luthans, F. (1977). *Organizational behavior* (2nd ed.). New York:
McGraw-Hill.

Lynch, R. (1984). Preparing an effective recruitment campaign. In R.
Lynch (Ed.), *Voluntary action leadership, Vol. 2* (pp. 1–6). Arlington, VA: National Volunteer Center.

Margolis, F. H., & Bell, C. R. (1986). *Instructing for results*. Minnea-
polis, MN: Lakewood.

Maslow, A. H. (1970). *Motivation and personality* (2nd ed.). New
York: Harper & Row.

Masnerie, C. G. (1996). *A comparison of the leadership practices of
key administrators in non-profit human services organizations with
those of key administrators in for-profit businesses*. Unpublished
doctoral dissertation, Indiana University of Pennsylvania.

McKnight, J. S. (1995). *Toward a grounded, substantive theory of the
control of learning in altruistic grassroots initiatives*. Ann Arbor,
MI: UMI Dissertation Services.

Merriam, S. B., & Brockett, R. G. (1997). *The profession and practice of adult education: An introduction*. San Francisco: Jossey-Bass.

Miall, H. (1992). *The peacemakers: Peaceful settlement of disputes since 1945*. New York: St. Martin's Press.

Morrison, J. L. (1993, April). *Environmental scanning in educational planning: Establishing a strategic trend information system*. Paper presented at the Annual Meeting of the American Educational Research Association, Atlanta, GA. (ERIC Document Reproduction Service No. ED 361 897).

Mott Foundation (1975). *2 + 2 = 6 — Interagency cooperation*. (Film Services for Community Education Development). Produced in Flint, MI.

Murk, P. J. (1992). *The funding process: Grantwriting and research proposal manual*. Muncie, IN: Ball State University, Educational Leadership Department (unpublished manuscript).

Murk, P. J. (1994). Addressing community interagency cooperation. *Economic Development Review, 12*(5), 61–62.

Murk, P. J., & Galbraith, M. W. (1986). Planning successful continuing education programs: A systems approach model. *Lifelong Learning, 9*(5), 21–23.

Murk, P. J., & Stephan, J. F. (1994). Volunteers — how to get them, train them and keep them. *Michigan Middle School Journal, 19*(1), 18 & 208–220.

Murk, P. J., & Walls, J. L. (1996). The program planning wheel: The son of S.A.M. In J. M. Dirkx (Ed.), *Proceedings at the Midwest Research-to-Practice Conference in Adult, Continuing, and Community Education* (pp. 123–128). Lincoln, NE: University of Nebraska-Lincoln.

Nanus, B. (1989). *The leadership edge: Seven keys to leadership in a turbulent world*. New York: Contemporary.

Nilson, C. (1993). *Team games for trainers*. New York: McGraw-Hill.

Nonaka, I., & Takeuchi, H. (1995). *The knowledge-creating company*. New York: Oxford University Press.

Pennington, F., & Green, J. (1976). Comparative analysis of program development process in six professions. *Adult education, 27*(1), 12–23.

Peters, T., & Waterman, R. H. (1982). *In search of excellence: Lessons from America's best run companies*. New York: Harper Collins.

Pfeiffer, J. W., & Jones, J. E. (Eds.). (1983). *A handbook of structured experiences from human relations training*. San Diego, CA: Pfeiffer & Company.

Pfeiffer, S. I. (1981). The status of training in school psychology and trends toward the future. *Journal of School Psychology, 19*(3), 211–216.

Pigors, P. W. (1935). *Leadership for domination.* Boston, MA: Houghton-Mifflin.

Plambeck, D. (1985). *Tips for training volunteers.* Washington, DC: National Academy for Volunteerism, The United Way of America.

Reddin, W. J. (1970). *Managerial effectiveness.* New York: McGraw-Hill.

Richards, A. (1979). *Managing volunteers for results.* (2nd ed.). San Francisco: Public Management Institute.

Roberts, N. (1985). Tranforming leadership: A process of collective action. *Human Relations, 38*(11), 1023–1046.

Ryan, J., & Townsend, K. A. (1992). Leadership in a changing environment. *Journal of Continuing Education, 40* (1), 29–33.

Sandole, D., & Van der Merwe, H. (1993). *Conflict resolution theory and practice: Integration and application.* New York: St. Martin's Press.

Scannell, E. E., & Newstrom, J. W. (1980). *Games trainers play.* New York: McGraw-Hill.

Scannell, E. E., & Newstrom, J. W. (1983). *More games trainers play.* New York: McGraw-Hill.

Schein, E. H. (1985). *Organizational culture and leadership.* San Francisco: Jossey-Bass.

Schein, E. H. (1992). *Organizational culture and leadership* (2nd ed.). San Francisco: Jossey-Bass.

Schindler-Rainman, E., & Lippitt, R. (1975). *The volunteer community: Creative use of human resources.* Fairfax, VA: NTL Learning Resources Corporation.

Schmidt, J. W. (1987). The leaders role in strategic planning. In R. G. Simerly & Associates (Eds.), *Strategic planning and leadership in continuing education* (pp. 31–50). San Francisco: Jossey-Bass.

Schroeder, W. L. (1970). Adult education defined and described. In R. M. Smith, G. F. Aker, & J. R. Kidd (Eds.), *Handbook of adult education* (pp. 25–44). New York: Macmillan.

Scott, R. W. (1981). *Organizations: Rational, natural, and open systems.* Englewood Cliffs, NJ: Prentice-Hall.

Senge, P. J. (1990). *The fifth discipline: The art and practice of the learning organization.* New York: Doubleday/Currency.

Shoop, R. J. (1984). *Developing interagency cooperation.* Midland, MI: Pendell.

Simerly, R. G. (1987a). Why continuing education leaders must plan strategically. In R. G. Simerly & Associates (Eds.), *Strategic planning and leadership in continuing education* (pp. 1–11). San Francisco: Jossey-Bass.

Simerly, R. G. (1987b). The strategic planning process: Seven essential steps. In R. G. Simerly & Associates (Eds.), *Strategic planning and leadership in continuing education* (pp. 12–30). San Francisco: Jossey-Bass.

Simerly, R. G. (1991). Preparing for the 21st century: Ten critical issues for continuing education. *The Journal of Continuing Higher Education, 39*(2), 2–12.

Smith, D. H. (1981). Altruism, volunteers and volunteering. *Journal of Voluntary Action Research, 10,* 21–36.

Sofo, F. (1995). *CReST: Critical reflection strategies using teams.* McKellar, Australia: F & M Sofo Educational Assistance.

Sork, T. J., & Buskey, J. H. (1986). A descriptive evaluative analysis of program planning literature, 1950–1983, *Adult Education Quarterly, 36* (2), 86–95.

Sork, T. J. & Caffarella, R. S. (1989). Planning programs for adults. In S. B. Merriam & P. M. Cunningham (Eds.), *Handbook of adult and continuing education* (pp. 233–245). San Francisco: Jossey-Bass.

Stenzel, K. S., & Feeny, H. M. (1976). *Volunteer training and development: A manual.* New York: Seabury Press.

Stodgill, R. M. (1964). *Handbook of leadership: A survey of theory and research.* New York: The Free Press.

Stone, J. M. (1982). *How to volunteer in social service agencies.* Springfield, IL: Charles C. Thomas.

Tyler, R. W. (1949). *Basic principles of curriculum and instruction.* Chicago: University of Chicago Press.

Vaill, P. B. (1996). *Learning as a way of being: Strategies for survival in a world of permanent white water.* San Francisco: Jossey-Bass.

Van Ness, R. H. (1981). *Agency collaboration for optimum results.* Muncie, IN: Ball State University, Community Education Development Center.

Van Ness, R. H. (1989). *Volunteering: A national profile* (1989). Arlington, VA: The National Volunteer Center.

Van Ness, R. H. (1992). *A dozen principles of managing people.* Muncie, IN: Ball State University, The School of Continuing Education and Public Service.

Van Ness, R. H. (1998a). *Contrasting traditional and new boards.*

(Available from Gem Associates, 1405 Briar Road, Muncie, IN, 47304, (765) 284-9534).

Van Ness, R. H. (1998b). *Harmonious board-staff relationships.* (Available from Gem Associates, 1405 Briar Road, Muncie, IN, 47304, (765) 284-9534).

Vroom, V. H., & Yetton, P. (1973). *Leadership and decision making.* Pittsburgh, PA: University of Pittsburgh Press.

Weihrich, H., & Koontz, H. (1993). *Management: A global perspective* (10th ed.). New York: McGraw Hill.

Wlodkowski, R. J. (1986). *Enhancing adult motivation to learn.* San Francisco: Jossey-Bass.

Wood, G. S. (1989). *State plan for Indiana community education, 1989–1993.* Muncie, IN: Ball State University, Department of Educational Leadership.

Zengler, C. J. (1998). Recent publications. *PAACE Journal of Lifelong Learning, 7,* 93–97.

INDEX